THE CRAFTSMAN'S ART SERIES

The Craft of Flower Arrangement

By the same author

Creative Flower Arrangement
Planting for Pleasure
The Garden Indoors (with William Davidson)

The Craftsman's Art Series

The Craft of
Flower
Arrangement

Jean Taylor

Stanley Paul, London

Stanley Paul & Co Ltd
3 Fitzroy Square, London W1

An imprint of the Hutchinson Publishing Group

London Melbourne Sydney Auckland
Wellington Johannesburg and agencies
throughout the world

First published 1976
© Jean Taylor 1976
Illustrations © Stanley Paul & Co Ltd 1976

Printed in Great Britain by The Anchor Press Ltd
and bound by Wm Brendon & Son Ltd, both of
Tiptree, Essex

ISBN 0 09 126770 6 (cased)
      0 09 126771 4 (paper)

Contents

Acknowledgements

My thanks are due to Douglas Rendell for taking the photographs and to my daughter Meredith for her help, as a beginner in flower arrangement.

Introduction

Flower arrangement is an easy and enjoyable subject to learn and one that can be practised at home. You need no special talent and no expensive equipment. The materials are cheap and easy to get and collecting them can be fascinating.

Outside the home there are now many opportunities to learn more about flower arranging and to enjoy it with other people, such as at flower clubs and colleges of further education.

You need no starting knowledge to understand this book. It begins with ordinary household equipment and explains the basic mechanical skills and simple design principles. It takes you a step beyond that of a beginner.

After reading the book and practising the suggested arrangements of flowers and leaves you should be able to arrange a variety of styles in your home. You should also have progressed beyond the stage of being a beginner and be ready to learn more about design and to achieve further skill in some of the techniques.

What you can achieve

Your achievements should include being able to:

Arrange flowers and leaves in easily available containers without special equipment, using ordinary household resources.

Support stems firmly in containers using water-retaining foam and pinholders.

Arrange flowers in a variety of containers for different positions in your home.

Handle flower scissors.

Arrange flowers for a table for a seated meal, including the uses of candles with flowers.

Know how to trim and clean plant material and keep it fresh for as long as possible, including both florist's and garden flowers.

Know what equipment to look for and collect. Know what plant material to look for, collect and grow.

Preserve and dry plant material for use when fresh plant material is scarce.

Clean, colour and polish driftwood and support it in an arrangement.

Know something about how to select suitable sizes, colours, shapes and textures and to be more aware of these qualities in everyday things about you.

Achieve good balance in a design and display your arrangements well.

Make arrangements of plant material in several styles: including the geometric styles of a triangle, Hogarth curve, crescent; free-form designs; landscape and Flemish flower-painting arrangements.

Make a cone of dried plant material, a simple fruit arrangement and prepare plant material for Christmas arrangements.

Make a pot-et-fleur to include house plants and cut flowers.

Most important – begin to create your own styles.

Flower arrangement is an art with achievements well within most people's reach. This book has been written to help you learn and enjoy it.

1. A Bunch of Flowers

Buy a bunch of flowers and take it home to enjoy or pick a handful in the garden. You may be surprised at the lively and colourful effect flowers give to your room and you will probably have a cheerful feeling every time you look at them because flowers make a room look cared for and lived in.

You should place the ends of the stems in deep water straight away because if they are left out of water for long the flowers and leaves wilt, becoming floppy. They can be put into a jug or bucket, almost full of tepid water, while you look for a more attractive container. Before placing the flowers in the bucket, snip off about *half an inch* of the stem using household scissors. This removes any seal that may have formed over the end of the stem during the time the flowers have been out of water. (A seal prevents the stems from taking up the water in the bucket.) Then cut the string or remove any ties and loosen the flowers.

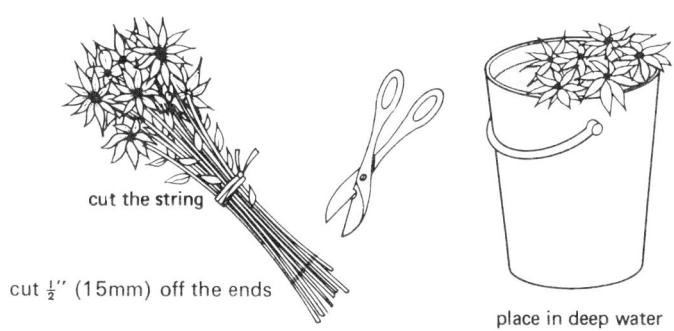

cut the string

cut $\frac{1}{2}''$ (15mm) off the ends

place in deep water

Arranging flowers without special equipment

You can make the flowers look attractive without having any special flower arranging equipment but stems need some support, otherwise they fall around and the flowers cannot be seen clearly. If you

The flowers are held in position because the stems fill the opening of the jug. The dahlias are turned to face different ways.

have a vase and the normal household resources then you can support stems and arrange flowers.

A jug

A jug is quite adequate if you completely fill the opening with stems so that they hold each other in place. Move the stems around so that each flower has a little space and turn the flowers to face different directions. This is more interesting than seeing the flowers all facing the same way. If the stems are tightly wedged in the neck of the jug you may be able to pull up some stems so that the flowers are separated and can be seen easily. A wide-necked jug needs many stems to fill it and this can be expensive unless you fill the jug first with leaves, then add a few flowers.

A narrow-necked vase

A vase that has a long, narrow neck is ideal because the neck supports the flowers and you do not need many stems to fill it. Fill the

Garden lilies and Hosta leaves are supported by the narrow neck of the container. One flower is pulled upwards.

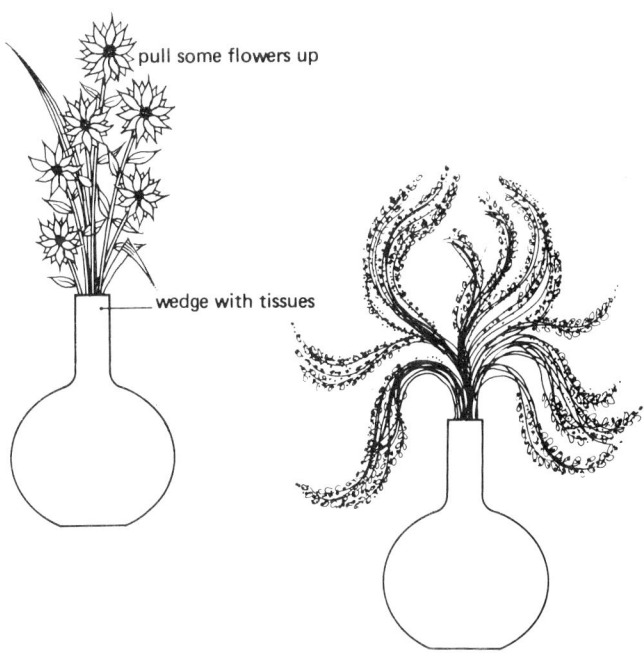

pull some flowers up

wedge with tissues

vase almost up to the top with water and then put all the stems in together in a bunch. Remove one or two if there is insufficient room. Curved stems are lovely because they droop down gracefully. If you have long straight stems you may need to pull up some, or shorten a few with scissors, in order to separate the flowers so that each can be seen. If the stems wobble about in the container they can be wedged in place with crumpled tissues pushed down into the neck.

A tall straight-sided vase

Tall vases with straight sides and wider openings can be filled with woody twigs cut from a shrub or tree. Take off any lower leaves because they become slimy under water and make it smell. Fill the vase about half full of twigs. Then, using household scissors, cut the tops level with the rim of the container so that they do not show. Put the flower stems in one at a time. The twigs should give them support. Add more twigs if the flower stems continue to wobble about, or remove a few if there is not enough room for the flower stems.

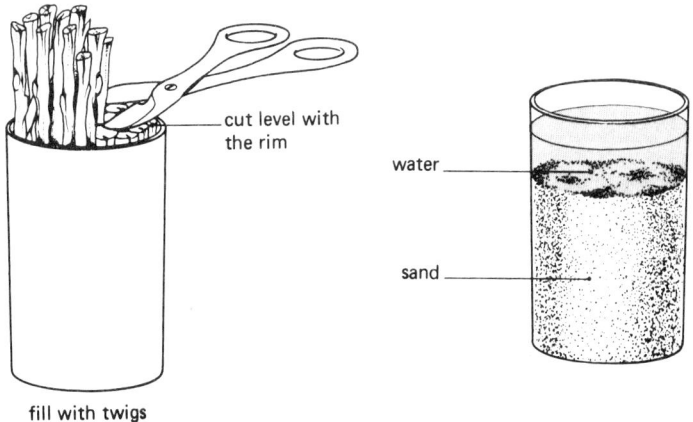

cut level with the rim

water

sand

fill with twigs

Sand, or gravel, will give slight support to stems in this type of container. Fill the vase two thirds of the way up with sand. Pour water into the vase until it stops gurgling and stands on top of the sand. If you have no sand or gravel and the container is too deep for the stems, pack the bottom of the vase inside with crumpled news-paper. This method can also be used, without water, to support the lightweight stems of dried flowers.

Sticky tape will support stems. Criss-cross it over the top of the vase to form square spaces. A stem can be placed in each space. Make certain that the surface of the container is quite dry on the outside or the tape will not stick. Leave spaces about half an inch square for thick stems and smaller for thin stems. The tape need only be stuck down to about half an inch on the outside of the container. If it looks unattractive find a leaf or flower with a curved stem to place over it and put some leaves over the tape in the centre.

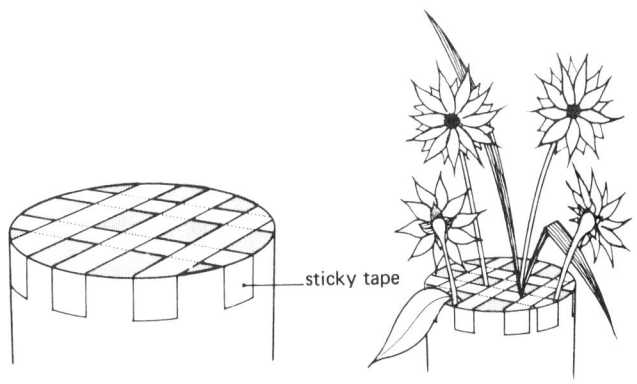

sticky tape

Flowers and leaves are supported by criss-crossed sticky tape.

A baking dish

Two or three large, round flowers such as peonies or roses can be floated on water in a shallow baking dish. Cut off the stems and place the flower heads on the water. Add one or two leaves to soften the appearance, with a few stones or shells for interest.

Wide vases and bowls

It takes many flowers to fill the large opening of a wide vase or bowl so that the stems are wedged in position. When you only have a few stems they lean against the side of the container leaving a gap in the centre and this is not as attractive as seeing flowers in the centre. The flowers also tend to slip sideways and cannot be clearly seen. Some form of support is necessary to hold the stems where you want them.

One method of doing this is to use the sticky tape technique already described. Use round flowers to fill the lattice of spaces. This shape conceals the tape and fills up the opening. Cut the stems the same length, or a little shorter, than the depth of the container so that the flower-heads are supported by the lattice-work of tape.

Another method of supporting stems, in a deeper bowl with a wide opening, is by means of a jam jar placed in the centre to reduce the space. Fill it with water and place the stems in the jar instead of in the outer container.

Our ancestors used 'roses' in bowls. These were glass mounds with holes in them and a stem-end could be placed in each hole. You can sometimes find these in antique shops but they are not made nowa-

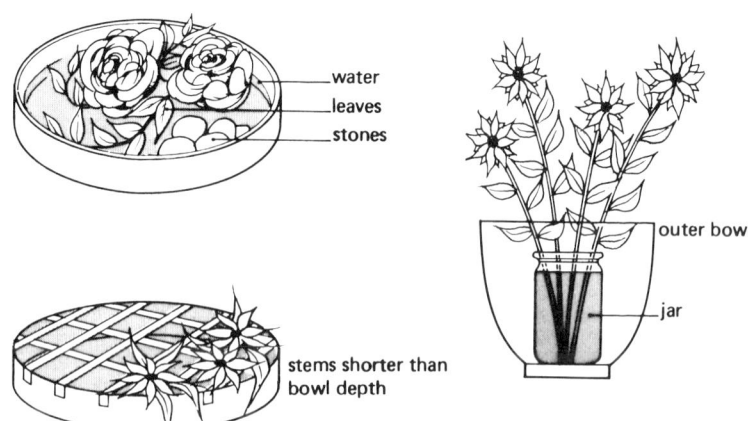

water
leaves
stones

outer bowl

jar

stems shorter than
bowl depth

days. A substance called plastic foam now does the same job and is more adaptable because the stems can be placed in any position.

Flower arranging with water-retaining foam

This remarkable substance has revolutionized the arranging of flowers and has made it so much quicker and easier. The plastic foam, sold under trade names such as Oasis and Bloomfix, is porous and has the power of taking up water and retaining it. Stems can be pushed into it very easily at any angle and can take up water from it. All but soft bendy stems will go into the foam and remain exactly where they are placed.

It is very light in weight when dry but becomes heavy when fully saturated with water. This means that it does not slip about easily in a vase. There are also methods of anchoring it if necessary. Blocks of foam are sold in a number of sizes and shapes. They are usually green in colour to make them less noticeable. They can be cut with a household knife when wet or dry to fit any vase. One drawback is that the foam is not a permanent support that can be used over and over again because the stem makes holes in it. These remain because the foam does not draw together again. Eventually it looks like a sponge and cannot support stems. However a 'round' – measuring approximately three inches (8 cm) in diameter and two and a half inches (6 cm) deep, which is adequate for a small arrangement and often can be used twice – costs about the same as a cup of coffee. It is well worth the small expense because it is so easy to use.

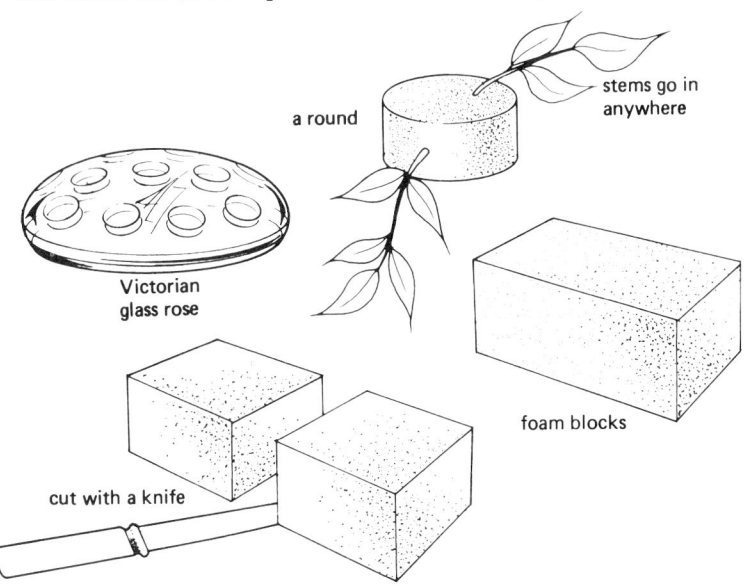

a round

stems go in anywhere

Victorian glass rose

cut with a knife

foam blocks

A simple table arrangement of roses and their leaves. The stems are supported by plastic foam placed in a saucer on a small wooden mat. A few rose-buds give a variety in shape.

A table arrangement

Try using plastic foam for supporting the stems of a small arrangement for the centre of a table. You may like to do this on an occasion when you invite friends to share a meal. Flowers give a festive feeling and look attractive in the table centre but often there is little time to fiddle about with them when you have a meal to prepare. Plastic foam can be filled with flowers and leaves to make an arrangement very quickly.

Buy from a florist:

1 *A small bunch of flowers* in a colour that suits your room and china. The flowers should be of medium size, about two and a half inches (6 cm) in diameter, such as roses, single chrysanthemums

(several small flowers on a stem and like a large daisy) or carnations. All these are available all the year round. Chrysanthemum blooms (one flower on a stem) are too large for a normal table.

2 *Some leaves* if the stems of the flowers look bare.

3 *A small round of plastic foam* for fresh flowers. There is also a type for dried stems that does not hold water.

If you have a garden you can pick a bunch of flowers and some leaves instead of buying them.

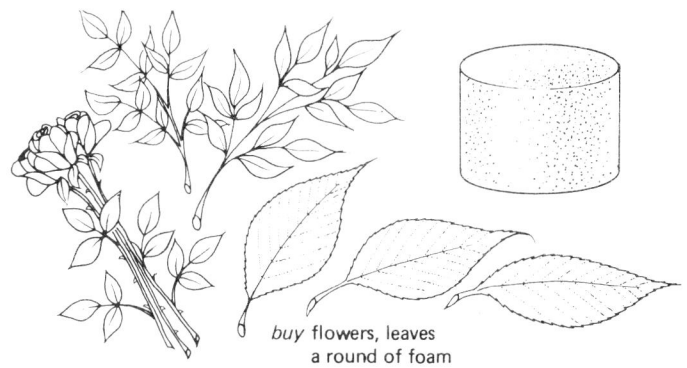

buy flowers, leaves
a round of foam

Preparation Put your flowers and leaves temporarily in water and place the round of foam into a bowl or saucepan of cold water. This should be deeper than the depth of the foam. At first the round will bob about on the surface but there is no need to push it under because it will gradually sink as water is taken up. This takes about *five minutes*. It is fully saturated when the round has sunk level with the top of the water. Any time after this it is ready to use. It can never take up *too much* water if left for longer. When you take it out of the bowl or saucepan, it will drip water so take a saucer, a small dish or an ashtray to it. Place this underneath the foam which can remain on the saucer when placed eventually in the centre of the dining table.

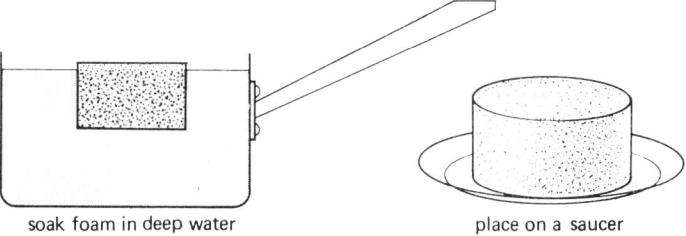

soak foam in deep water   place on a saucer

The stems of spray chrysanthemums may be cut to give separate flowers. This arrangement is supported by foam in an ashtray.

Before starting to put the flower stems into the foam spread a sheet of newspaper, or a length of polythene, on your work table. This speeds tidying up afterwards as any bits can be lifted up together and dropped into a waste bin. Newspaper or polythene also protects the table top if necessary from water spillage or scratching.

Place your household scissors; the saucer holding the foam; the flowers and leaves on the newspaper and sit down in front of them. This is a relaxing way to arrange flowers.

Making the arrangement   If the flowers are to be used on a table for a seated meal the arrangement should be no more than about eight inches (20 cm) tall, otherwise it is difficult for people to talk across the table and over the flowers. The stems of the flowers you

ready to start

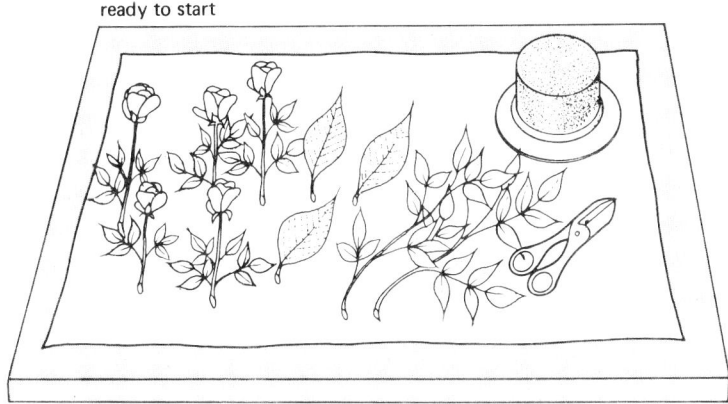

have bought will probably be longer than this so cut them to lengths of about three to four inches (8–10 cm).

The foam and saucer are not especially attractive to look at and are better hidden. It is extravagant and unnecessary to hide them with flowers: leaves are more suitable. They cover well when their stems are cut short and they also provide a plain background for showing up the more decorative flowers.

There may be some leaves left on the stems you have cut from the flowers, otherwise use leaves bought separately from the florist or pick a few in the garden. Flat ones with strong stems are the easiest to use, such as large ivy, geranium or laurel leaves.

Cut the stems off the leaves so that they are about one inch long and push them into the foam. You will find that they go in easily. Push them in for about half an inch (1 cm) or until they seem firm. Place the stems into the foam at a sideways angle so that the leaves

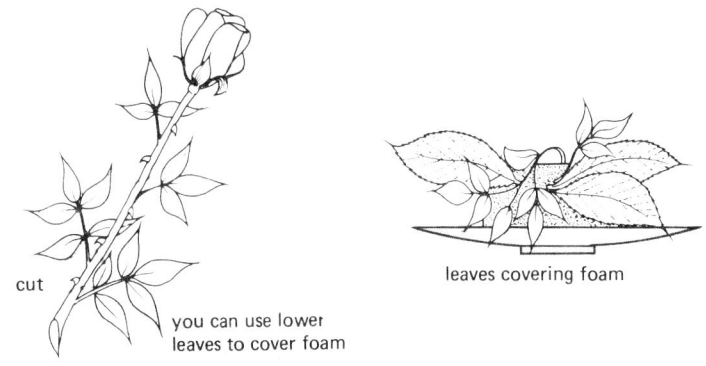

cut

you can use lower
leaves to cover foam

leaves covering foam

cover more foam than if you put the stems in straight. There is no need to cover the foam closely because its green colour will blend in with the foliage. It is now time to add the flowers.

Each flower is 'a star performer' and should be clearly seen because the flowers are the main decoration. Leave some space around each one, as you push the stems into the foam in any position you like. Lift a leaf if it is in the way and place the flower stem behind it. If you have a garden you may like to add a few more flowers or leaves, between those already used.

The design The flowers can be placed in various positions. You can put a flower in the centre standing upright, and the other flowers around it facing different ways. Alternatively start with a flower in the centre and then add the others in steps downwards, with each flower stem cut a little shorter than the one before. The arrangement will look better if the ends of the flower stems are placed close together, so that the flowers radiate as the spokes of a bicycle wheel, instead of standing parallel to each other. If you have spare leaves they can be placed in between the flowers.

place stem ends together

not apart

Try not to keep on putting stems into the foam and then taking them out because this makes lots of holes, the flowers begin to look tired and you get irritable. Remember that flowers do not last a long time and it is better to arrange them quickly and then leave them alone. If you are not entirely happy with the result you can try another way of arranging them next time.

When you have finished the arrangement, wipe the bottom of the saucer, in case it is damp, before placing the flowers on the table. You can put the saucer on to a small mat to protect the table top if you think it necessary.

After-care   A dribble of water should be poured on to the top of the foam every other day (every day in a hot, dry room) to keep it moist. You can do this with a jug but it is easier to use a small watering can with a long spout. Alternatively carry the arrangement to the sink and pour on a little water from the tap.

When the flowers die, throw them away. The foliage may still look fresh and new flowers can be added. The foam may be used several times depending on the number of stems that are used. If a lot of flowers and leaves have been placed in the block then it can only be used once. If only a few stems have been inserted, the foam can be turned upside down in the saucer (so that the holes are at the bottom) and used again. If you do not intend re-using the foam immediately, remove it from the saucer and place it in a small polythene bag to keep it damp. If it dries out completely it may not take up water again. When you wish to use it again, remove it from the bag and drop it into deep water for a few minutes before arranging flowers in it once more.

Try different positions for the flower stems each time you do an arrangement but *place leaves in first* to hide the foam.

Candles and flowers

Candles are often used in winter on a dining table and an attractive arrangement can be made with flowers placed around a short, wide candle. Place the candle on top of a round of foam in a saucer, ashtray or small dish. Then add flowers and leaves around the candle. Few are needed if you put the leaves in first and then add round flowers such as single chrysanthemums.

Tall candles in a pair of candlesticks can be decorated with flowers quickly and easily for a party. Cut a round block of foam in half lengthwise and push each half on to the pointed end of the candles and down on to the candlesticks. Do this on the draining board because they will drip water for a while. Cut the stems of the leaves and flowers about half an inch long (1 cm) and push them into the foam. When the dripping stops, place the candlesticks on the table. The flowers may not last for more than a day or two because it is difficult to water the foam but you can take them to the sink to pour on a little water.

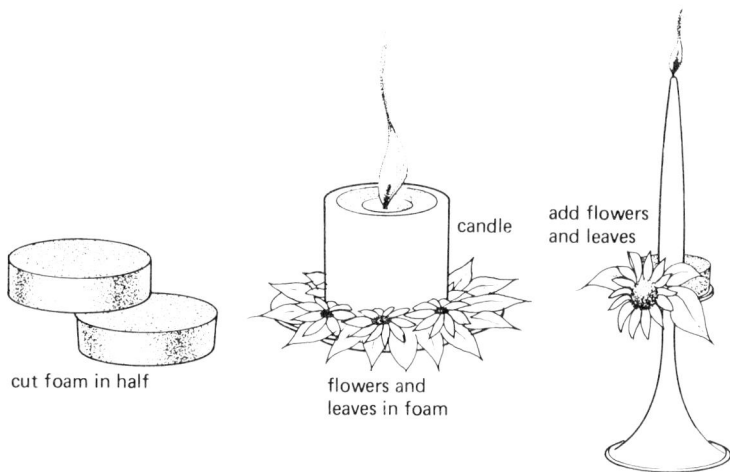

cut foam in half

candle

flowers and leaves in foam

add flowers and leaves

Anchoring foam

You may find that the block of foam moves about on a saucer. There are two ways of holding it more firmly in position, using equipment available from a florist.

1 *A plastic saucer* can be bought which is made especially to hold a round of foam. It fits tightly into it and so cannot move. Saucers are made normally in green, black or white and are inexpensive. They can be used over and over again and are big enough to catch drips of water but small enough to be easily hidden with leaves. White is too obvious a colour and green or black are better because they do not show among the flowers and leaves.

Flowers, leaves and candles are supported by plastic foam.

2 *A foam anchor* is a piece of equipment that holds the foam by means of sharp, widely-spaced pins, or prongs, about one and a half inches (4 cm) long. They pierce the foam and hold it firmly. The best ones are made of lead. This makes them heavy and so they stay in position in the container. If they do slide about they can be easily anchored with a little plasticine or sealing strip (such as Bostik).

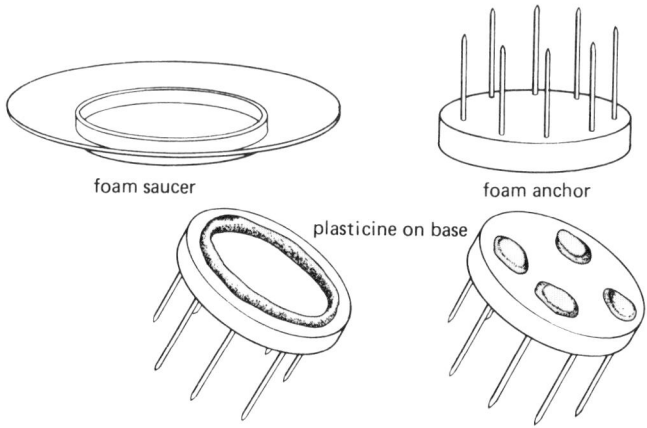

foam saucer   foam anchor

plasticine on base

Roll the plasticine into a small sausage, or into four small pellets, and press it on to the underneath of the anchor. Then push the anchor down on to the container giving a slight twist as you do so. It should then be quite firm. Make sure the plasticine, container and anchor are absolutely dry before doing this, otherwise the anchor will not stick down. When you wish to remove it from the container, twist and lift it in one movement, or force a thin-bladed knife underneath. The prongs are very sharp, so be careful and also keep the anchor away from children at all times.

An arrangement using foam in a baking dish

A foam anchor can be used to hold a block of foam in a wide container, such as a baking dish about ten to twelve inches long. A big arrangement to place on a side table, shelf or chest can be made in this type of container. A small round of foam is not big enough for many flowers or those with thick stems and it is better to use a larger block. Buy one measuring about nine inches (23 cm) by three inches (8 cm), by four and a half inches (12 cm). You need not fill the

An arrangement made in a small block of foam held in place by a foam anchor secured to the baking dish.

container with foam and it is rarely necessary to use a full block. Cut it in half with a kitchen knife *before* soaking and save the second half for another arrangement.

Place the soaked block of foam on an anchor which has been secured with plasticine. Then push in leaves, followed by flower stems used at any desired height. Cut some stems shorter than others so that the flowers finish at different levels. Place some flowers or leaves towards the back of the design for stability so that the foam will not tip forwards with the weight of the flowers.

Foam stands above the rim of the container so that some stems can flow downwards.

An arrangement using foam in an urn

Half a block or more of foam is excellent for supporting stems in an urn-shaped container when you want a large display of flowers. Cut it to a size that fits the container exactly but make sure that it stands about two inches (5 cm) above the top of the container because then you can place stems in it, to flow downwards. It is best to cut a little off the sides of the block (if necessary) and then to try it in the container and to continue to do this until it fits. If you cut it too small so that it wobbles around you can always use a foam anchor to hold it in position. Cover with leaves and then add flowers and more leaves if you wish.

What you have achieved so far   By this time you should be able to support and arrange flowers in a jug, narrow-necked vase, or bowl; to make a simple arrangement for a table centre, using plastic foam; to do a bigger arrangement using foam in a baking dish or an urn. You may now like to try an arrangement using fewer leaves and flowers.

Arrangements with few flowers and leaves

Foam is very easy and quick to use but it needs many leaves to cover it and consequently arrangements supported with it tend to be rather full of plant material. Sometimes you may enjoy a sparse arrangement especially in winter when flowers are expensive and leaves difficult to get. Arrangements using a lot of space within the design and little plant material cannot be arranged without support for the stems. A pinholder is the answer. This is a disc of lead with sharp pins about three quarters of an inch (2 cm) long. Stems can be impaled on the sharp pins or placed between them. It is ideal for bare branches and strong stems. It is no use for thin stems which slip between the pins and are not held in place. It is not possible to put stems in at a sharp angle, as in foam, but it is much easier to conceal.

It is well worth getting a pinholder of good quality. It may be an expensive piece of equipment to buy (£1 to £3) in the first place but it lasts indefinitely and does not need replacement. It should be heavy, rustproof and about three inches (8 cm) in diameter. The pins should be long and set close together. Most florists stock pinholders or will obtain one for you.

The weight usually holds it in position in a container but it can be anchored down with plasticine in the same way as a foam anchor (which is similar but has pins set wider apart). It can be used with success in a baking dish.

Try pushing a stem down on to the pins and see how well it stays in place. If you wish to angle the stem push it straight on to the pinholder and then with your fingers on the lowest part of the stem press it gently in the desired direction.

In the winter try a design with two or three branches, two flowers and a few leaves, using a pinholder in a baking dish.

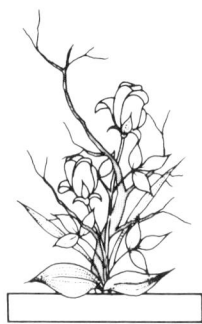

Making the arrangement   Fix the pinholder to one side of the container and place the end of a branch on to it towards the centre of

A pinholder supports a branch, laurel leaves and a spray of chrysanthemums cut into single stems in a baking dish.

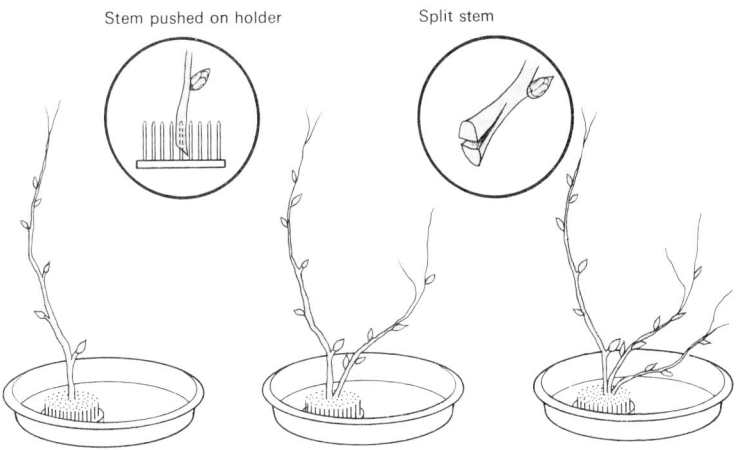

Stem pushed on holder　　　Split stem

the pinholder. It may be necessary to split the end about half an inch with a knife or scissors in order to get it on to the pinholder. Place the end of a second branch close to the first one and then press them both into position so that they are spaced apart. Add a third branch if you like. It is more interesting if all the stems are different lengths. Some people like the rough guide of the longest stem being about one and a half to two times the width of the container, but the eye is a good judge. Shorten the branches if you feel they are too tall for the container.

The branches may have many twigs on them and look muddly. This can detract from the design and it is better to remove some to give a more streamlined appearance. This is called trimming and it can be done before you place the branches on a pinholder, or afterwards, or both.

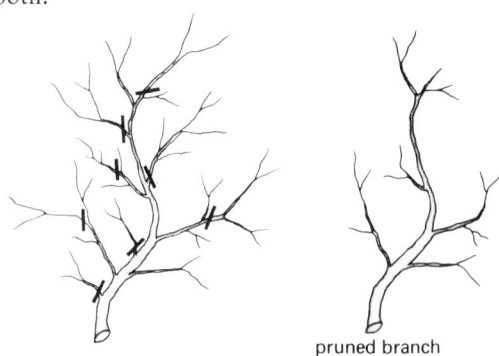

pruned branch

After the branches are positioned to your satisfaction look for a convenient space in which to place the flowers. They may look their best put fairly close together, with the stems slightly different lengths, about halfway between the top of the tallest branch and the bottom of the container or you can place them lower down.

Two or three leaves may then be added to soften the design but if there are many leaves on the flower stems further leaves may not be necessary. The pinholder will probably show at this stage but it can be concealed with a few stones.

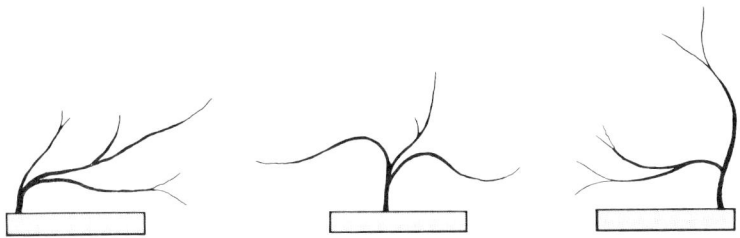

When the flowers are dead try the same branches arranged in different positions with some other variety of flower. This is an economical arrangement and should give great pleasure because you can study every piece of plant material in the uncrowded design. With the same type of branches, flowers and leaves try different lengths of stem, varying numbers of flowers and leaves, different positions for everything. Also experiment to find out how little plant material is necessary to make an interesting and decorative design.

The pinholder that you have used in this arrangement can also be used to hold flower stems in a tall, straight-sided container containing sand. Fill the vase two thirds of the way up with sand and pour in water to the top, adding more until clear water stands on the top of the sand. Drop in the pinholder.

All supports for plant material, including foam and pinholders, are known as 'mechanics'.

Equipment for flower arrangement

You will be able to make a variety of designs with the equipment already suggested, which you may have bought or owned before. In addition, flower scissors and several bases are helpful.

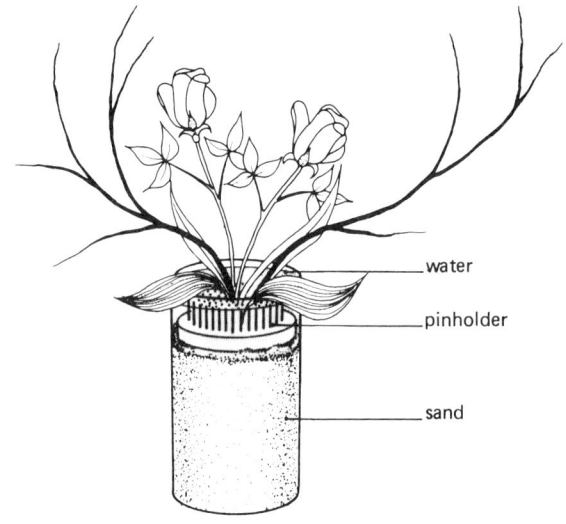

water

pinholder

sand

Flower scissors

Flower scissors are a good investment if you have decided to continue arranging flowers in your home. They are stocked by florists. The blades are short and have blunt ends. One edge is serrated to make cutting stems easier. There is also a small nick at the base for cutting lightweight wire. Flower scissors are light, easy to handle and cut all but thick, woody stems for which heavier secateurs are necessary. To keep them in good condition you should regularly oil the blades and the part where they join.

Bases

A variety of effects can be achieved by the use of 'a base' and you need not rush to buy any more containers until you see one you especially like. 'A base' is really a mat such as the type used under hot dishes on a table. Such mats are in fact suitable. A base is useful for two reasons:

It protects your furniture from water damage and can be placed under any container for this purpose.

It can be used under a small, concealed container, such as a foam saucer, ashtray, dish or empty food tin containing plastic foam or a pinholder. The mat extends the container and makes the bottom of the design look more finished and important.

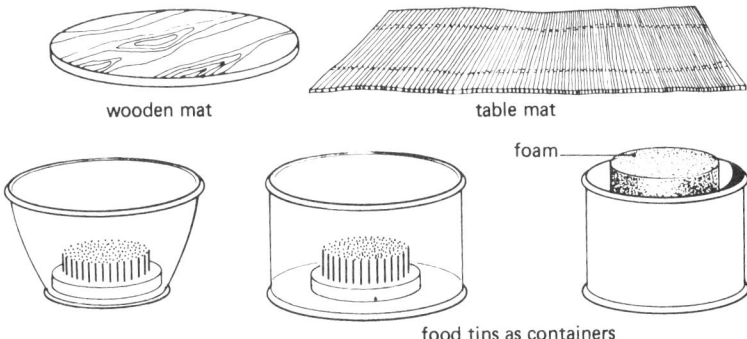

Daffodils, winter jasmine and ivy leaves arranged on a pinholder or in foam inside a food tin. The base is an upturned wooden plate.

wooden mat   table mat

foam

food tins as containers

Suitable bases are wooden, straw or plastic table mats.

Concealed containers should be deep enough to hold plenty of water for the plant material. If they look shiny or conspicuous they can be painted with mat black, or dark green, or brown emulsion paint.

You should now be able to make a wide variety of flower arrangements with the following equipment:

a foam saucer	several bases
plastic foam blocks	food tins
a narrow-necked vase	an urn
a straight-sided container	a bucket
a bowl	a baking dish
a jug	a pinholder
a foam anchor	flower scissors

Simple guidelines for arranging

When arranging flowers there are some simple guidelines to think about:

1 You can see the shape of the flowers better when they are not squashed together. *Separate the flowers* to give some space around each one. Japanese flower arrangers suggest that you should leave room for the butterflies to fly through.

2 It is more interesting if you can see the flowers at different angles so *turn the flower heads* to face in all ways to get a variety of views. Often the design looks better if the flowers in the centre face forward and the others turn gradually away from the centre on each side.

3 *Cut the stems different lengths* so that the flowers end up at different heights and this helps each one to be clearly seen.

4 Taking a long time to do the flowers does not necessarily make them look any better. Get into the habit of putting them into a container quickly and *do not 'labour' over an arrangement.* You can take a look in a spare moment to see if there is anything you might change next time. The flowers will have faded in about a week and so you can have another try with another bunch of flowers. It is important to enjoy what you do and to be spontaneous about it. Each time you make an arrangement you will do it more easily than the time before. Although the transient quality of flowers has its drawbacks, it also has the advantage of giving you continual opportunities to try different ways of arranging them.

5 *Leaves make an economical arrangement* and they are an excellent background for flowers. Begin a design by placing leaves in a container. Then add two, three or more flowers if you wish.

2. The Care of Flowers and Leaves

An arrangement looks so much better if the flowers look fresh and undamaged, the leaves are clean and there is no wilted plant material.

Grooming flowers and leaves

It never occurs to us when making a dress or curtains to use damaged fabric but sometimes a damaged flower or leaf slips into an arrangement. Snip them off with your flower scissors either before, or after, placing the stems in a container. Ragged edges can be trimmed off leaves without harming them. Beech leaves often have holes in them and these can be seen against the light. It is better to remove them from the branch.

Broken stems should also be cut away as the water will not travel along them and they wilt. Leaves, growing in cities, are sometimes dirty but they can be easily cleaned by swishing them about in slighly soapy, warm water. If this does not remove the dirt, wipe it off with wet tissues.

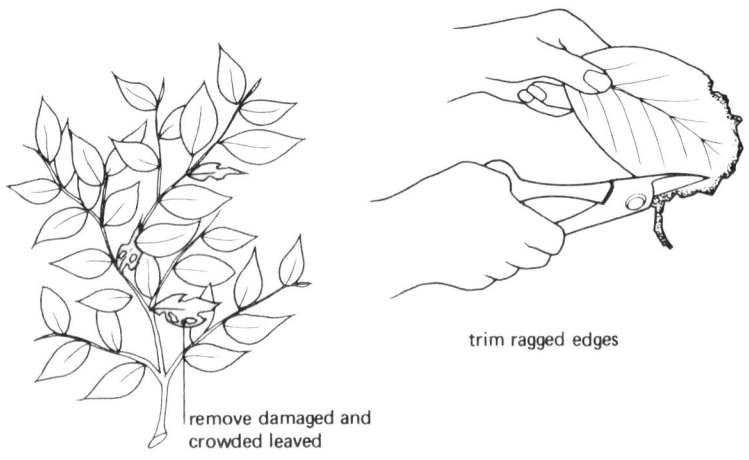

remove damaged and crowded leaved

trim ragged edges

Sometimes stems seem crowded with leaves and it is better to remove some of them for a tidier-looking design.

Wilted flowers

One or more flowers may wilt in an arrangement. This does not mean their life is over but it does mean that water is not travelling up the stems to hold them upright (or turgid). This happens for a variety of reasons:

1 The container may be without water or the foam may have dried out. This can be avoided by topping up with water every day or so using a long-spouted watering can.

2 A seal may have formed over the end of the stem to prevent the uptake of water. This could happen at a time when the flower stem was out of water. This is easily avoided if the stem ends are snipped off before being placed in water.

3 The flower may have many petals. In a dry room each one continually gives off water in the form of vapour and unless the water is replaced the petals become floppy. This is easier to understand if you think what happens to a line of wet washing. On a warm, dry or windy day the clothes give up their wetness and become dry. On a damp day they remain wet. Flowers and leaves dry out in a dry, warm or draughty atmosphere. They rarely do this in the garden because the atmosphere is much damper than in our dry living

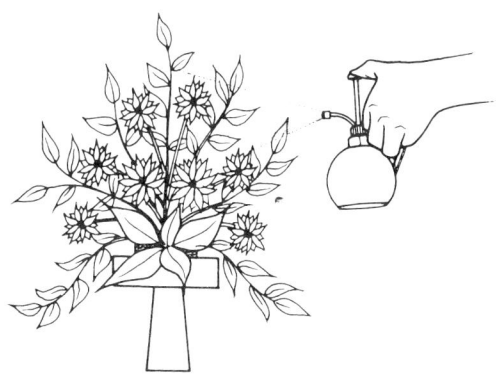

rooms. Although we provide water in a container the amount travelling up the thin stems is not enough to make up for the amount lost through the petals and leaves in a dry room. This process is called *transpiration*. It is a help to spray the arrangement, using a sprayer sold for houseplants. This makes the surrounding air less dry and lessens transpiration. The arrangement can be removed to a bathroom or kitchen for spraying, to avoid damage to wallpaper or furniture, but with care it can be sprayed where it stands.

4 The stem may carry many leaves which transpire in the same way as flowers. Remove some of the leaves to lessen this.

5 There may be a bubble of air in the stem which prevents water from rising. This can usually be avoided if you snip off half an inch (1 cm) of stem before placing it in water.

First-aid treatment

It is a pity to throw away a wilted flower as it can often be revived. Remove the stem from the arrangement, cutting it off, low down, if its removal would disturb the other flowers. Cut off an inch (2·5 cm) of the end (if not previously cut) and place the stem in deep, warm water for two or three hours in a cool, dimly-lit room.

Another method that works well with wilted roses, is to cut the stem end and then float the complete stem and flower on top of slightly warm water in a sink for two or three hours.

A third method is to place the end of the stem in two inches (5 cm) of very hot (just boiled) water. Leave the stem in the water until it cools and then fill up the jug with warm water and leave for two or three hours in a cool, dimly-lit room. The end of the stem may be floppy and useless when you come to rearrange the flowers, because boiling water destroys the cells in the stem, but simply cut off this part.

Preparing flowers to last longer

Flowers have a short life and nothing can prevent them from eventually fading but perhaps this is part of their beauty and makes them more precious to us. Their lives can be lengthened in the home by a little preparation before they are placed in an arrangement.

Shop flowers

Shop flowers have been prepared by the florist for a long life and they are ready to use at once. Also the cut flower trade specifically grows those that travel well and last a long time. It is only necessary to snip off the end of the stem before placing them in water.

It is sensible to buy young flowers and many buds are now sent to the markets. It is interesting to watch them gradually open into flowers and you will have longer to enjoy them. Florists do not knowingly sell old flowers but you should look for crisp leaves and light yellow centres. If the flower has many petals, like a chrysanthemum bloom, the centres should be tightly packed.

Garden flowers

In the garden choose young flowers that are showing colour and not those in tight bud or in full bloom. Avoid cutting in the middle of a hot day when the flowers may be limp but otherwise you can pick at any time. Take a bucket, half full of warm water, into the garden and put the stems into it immediately. Otherwise put them in water as soon as you get into the house, snipping off half an inch (1 cm) of stem as you place them in deep warm water in a bucket. Then place the bucket in a cool, dimly-lit place such as a garage or outhouse for two hours or overnight to make sure the stems are really full of water before they are arranged in a warm dry room.

Soaking in these conditions lessens transpiration. Warm water travels up the stems of the flowers more quickly than cold water and reaches the petals before they start to become limp.

Types of stems

Stems vary in structure and can be soft, hard or woody on the outside. Some stems are hollow and others contain a milky substance. Soft stems have no trouble in taking up water but hard and woody stems need preparation.

Hard stems Split the stem end for about an inch (2·5 cm) with a knife or flower scissors. This exposes the soft inner tissue which takes up water more rapidly. Roses and chrysanthemums need this treatment. More than one split may be necessary for thick stems.

Woody stems The woody outside bark is protective and prevents water from going either out or in. Remove an inch or two from the stem by scraping it off with a small kitchen knife. Then make one or two splits in the stem (as for hard stems). Lilac and many evergreens have this type of stem.

Hollow stems   You can fill hollow stems with water by turning them upside-down and filling them by means of a thin-spouted watering can. You may not feel it is worth the trouble as it can be messy but it does seem to help lupins, delphiniums and wide-stemmed dahlias. Place your finger over the end of the stem, or stuff it with tissues, before upturning it, otherwise the water will run out again.

Milky stems   Fortunately there are not many stems that contain a milky fluid but perennial poppies are an example. The milk is latex which dries at the stem end and prevents water from entering. (Latex can harm your eyes so do not rub them after handling such stems.) This seal can be prevented by holding the end of the stem over the flame of a gas jet, or match, until the sizzling stops. This should be repeated if the stem is recut.

The stems of all garden flowers should have a preliminary soak in deep water after the stem ends have been prepared. Leave them for a minimum of two hours or overnight. Choose a cool, dimly-lit place such as the garage or an outhouse. They should then be turgid (full of water) and ready to arrange.

Buckets

Ordinary household buckets can be used but florists sell deep ones especially for soaking flowers. Instead of a single, central handle which can knock off flower heads, they have two side handles which cannot damage the flowers.

Preparation of leaves

Foliage can be prepared for a longer life by soaking it in tepid water in a bucket, bowl or sink. This prevents transpiration while the leaves become really full of water. They can absorb it through their surfaces without damage. (The petals of flowers turn brown if left under water.) It is not advisable to submerge grey foliage as the tiny hairs that make it look grey become waterlogged and drip on to the furniture when placed in an arrangement.

After-care of arrangements

The life of a flower arrangement is affected by its position in a room.

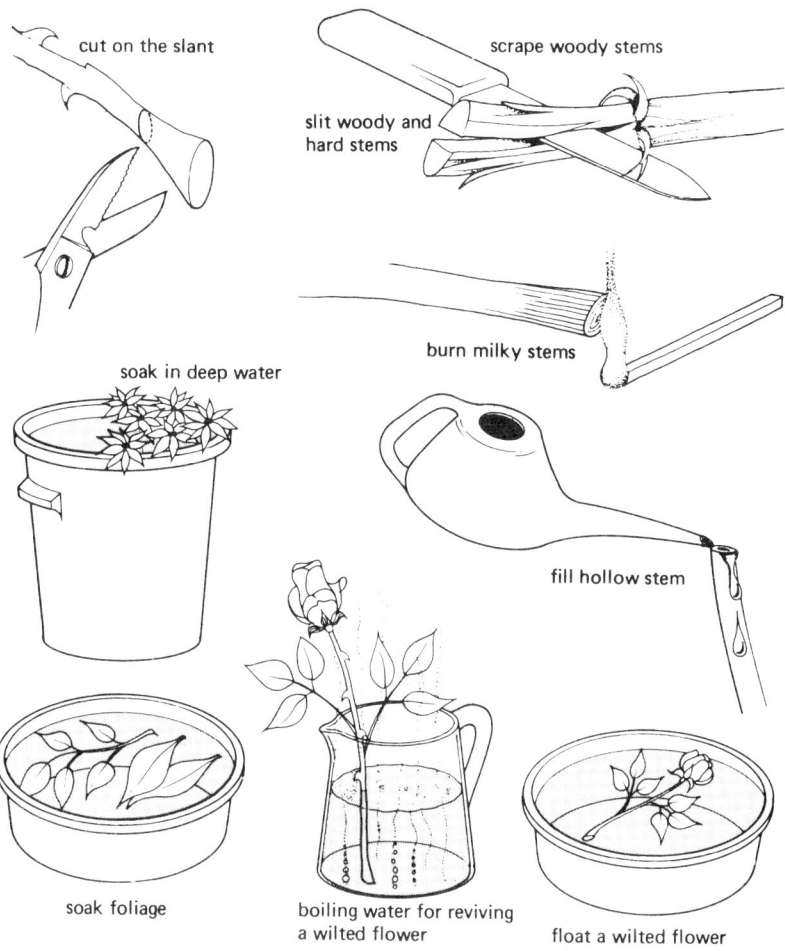

cut on the slant

scrape woody stems

slit woody and
hard stems

burn milky stems

soak in deep water

fill hollow stem

soak foliage

boiling water for reviving
a wilted flower

float a wilted flower

If it is hot and dry then wilting soon occurs. Avoid sunny windows, the top of the television set, the mantelpiece over the fire, the top of a radiator and draughty positions. In all these places the air is drier than in other parts of the room. If you want an arrangement to last, remove it to a cool place overnight.

Preparing stems and soaking them in water before arranging the flowers is called 'conditioning' by experienced flower arrangers.

3. The Materials for Flower Arrangement

Every art and craft has its own special materials and these are called 'the medium'. A sculptor's medium includes metal, wood and stone; a weaver uses the threads of textiles; an artist works with paints. The title 'flower arrangement' suggests a subject for which the medium is flowers. In recent years however this has become inadequate because the medium is now plant material of all kinds, at all stages of growth, both fresh and dried. This has considerably broadened the subject of flower arrangement.

Flowers, leaves, branches, driftwood, fruit, seedheads, bark, roots, bracts, grasses, ferns, nuts, cones, vegetables, catkins and seeds are used, alone or combined. Beautiful designs can be made of fruit and leaves, driftwood and seedheads, grasses and roots, and so on. There are no rules except in competitive work, and you should feel free to use any plant material that you like.

Making a collection

It is helpful to have a stock of plant material because simply by having it around you can be inspired to make an arrangement. Such objects as stones and pieces of driftwood to cover your pinholder are also useful. A collection need not be expensive and it can be built up gradually as you find things you like. Flower arrangers become like squirrels. They hoard all kinds of things that 'might come in handy' sometime for an arrangement. Containers are a necessity to enable stems to be placed in water and this means searching for interesting vases in shops, markets and potteries; plant material can be gathered in the country and by the sea-side; flowers, leaves and seedheads can be grown in a garden so that the flower arranger need not purchase materials every time; simple containers and bases can be made at home and plant material can be preserved and dried for use in winter. Collecting materials can be a most enjoyable interest and every visit to the country, sea or town can produce treasures to add to the hoard. Many of these can be obtained without cost.

Things to pick

We are asked not to pick wild flowers because of the need to conserve them but it does no harm to pick things that are plentiful. It is considerate to pick with restraint and care and to ask permission to do this on private ground. The following are useful:

dock	the brown, rough-textured seedheads grow on wasteland in autumn; hang to dry
grasses	many varieties grow on sandhills, wasteland, by lake and stream; hang to dry
bulrushes	these dry naturally but a little hairspray will keep them from blowing
seedheads	the autumn hedgerows yield seedheads such as Queen Anne's lace and cow-parsley which dry naturally
heather	this dries naturally
old-man's beard	growing mostly in the southern counties long trails drape the hedgerows
ivy	ivy can be picked all the year round both single leaves and trails
pussy willow, hazel, alder catkins	pick in the spring
moss	useful for covering mechanics
blackberries, hips and haws	sprays for arrangements in autumn
leaves turning colour	especially elderberry in autumn and sycamore in spring
beech leaves	collect in July for preserving
ferns and bracken	collect in a polythene bag as they soon go limp

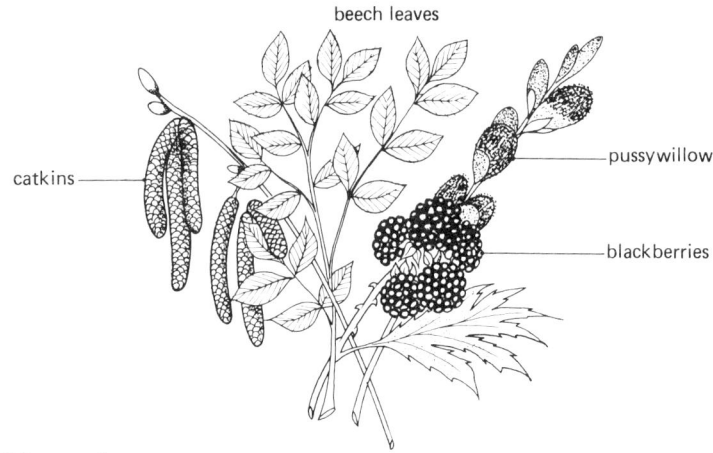

Things to buy

containers in markets, shops, potteries and craft studios
mats of raffia, straw and wood for bases, in kitchen and gift shops
candles in subtle colours to combine with flowers
fabric remnants to cover bases (see page 62).

Things to grow

Leaves

It is convenient to be able to cut leaves from plants growing in a garden. Plants grown for their leaves are a good investment. They provide a background for cut flowers and make it possible to economize on flowers. The smallest plot can grow enough leaves if you choose suitable plants.

Some leaves wilt easily when cut but there are many that last and can be arranged with fresh flowers several times over. The sooner planting takes place the better because it may take a few months for a plant to grow before you can cut leaves from it. The following plants are readily available, easy to grow and last well after being cut. They make a suitable starting collection. If possible plant three or four of a kind to give plenty of leaves.

Geraniums (zonal Pelargoniums), the outdoor type which is available from May in garden centres has useful round leaves that cover foam well. Plant in places that get the sun, in any soil. Discard in October, or cut down to about three inches and pot in John

Innes No. 2 potting compost. Keep on the dry side in a frost-free place and plant out again in May.

Honesty (*Lunaria annua*) is a quick-growing biennial (this means it takes two seasons to grow from seed and then dies). Buy seeds and plant them out-of-doors in a slightly shady position in May. Remove and discard some of the small plants if they are crowded. Small purple or white flowers appear the next April to June, followed by papery, silver seedheads (if the outer covering is removed). The heart-shaped leaves are excellent for general use all the year round and if a few seedheads are left on the plant, honesty will seed itself and save you the trouble of sowing.

Bergenia is an evergreen that can be picked all year, although ragged edges may need trimming in the winter. The oval, or round, leaves are large and flat with short stems. Any soil is suitable. The leaves sometimes turn red in winter. Plant several clumps together any time between October and March when the ground is not hard, in sun or partial shade. Preferably plant them in a raised bed, near a stone path or anywhere where the soil is well drained. There are several species of *Bergenia* which are useful but *B. purpurascens* is a good plant.

Hosta is a perennial (a plant that comes up every year) but it dies down each autumn. Leaves can be cut from May to October for general use in arrangements. Plant from October to March, when the ground is not hard, in sun or semi-shade. There are many species, and nurserymen sell collections of six to eight different species so that you may have a variety of leaf size. Some have plain green leaves but there are others marked with white, yellow and paler green colours. Useful plants are *H. crispula* (white margins), *H. sieboldiana* (large blue-green leaves), *H. elata* (large dark green leaves), *H. fortunei albopicta* (variegated pale green and yellow).

Solomon's seal (*Polygonatum x. hybridum*), a perennial with graceful arched stems of leaves, is very hardy and grows in any soil. Plant from September to March in partial shade.

Ivy, an evergreen climber with long trails, grows over a wall or fence or up a tree. Cut it back close to its support in February or March for attractive new growth. *Hedera colchica dentata* 'Variegata' is a strong variety with green and yellow leaves. *H. canariensis* 'Variegata' has green and grey leaves.

Iris has useful spear-like leaves which last for many months in the garden. The common, bearded irises are useful and also *I. pallida dalmatica*. Plant in late June with the rhizome just showing out of the soil, in full sun.

Lady's mantle (*Alchemilla mollis*) is a perennial with pale green, rounded leaves and small yellow-green flowers. The leaves are useful for covering foam and the flowers are good 'fillers' for using with other flowers. Plant from October to March, in sun.

Soft shield fern (*Polystichum setiferum*) is a hardy fern with a feathery-shaped leaf. Plant in April.

Evergreens

You may already have several in your garden but if not, and you have space, the following are decorative in the garden and useful for cutting. Plant in autumn or spring and cut sparingly for a year or two until they are established.

Elaeagnus pungens 'Variegata' or *Elaeagnus* 'Limelight', both have yellow-splashed leaves and *E. macrophylla* has grey-green leaves.

Golden privet with yellow-green foliage is useful if you do not clip it so that you have long sprays.

Fatsia japonica is a good shrub for town gardens and has large leaves with lobes like a hand. It grows in any soil, in sun or shade but does not like wind.

Mahonia x. 'Charity' has graceful sprays of leaves and can be planted in sun or shade. Cut off the top in spring to encourage new growth.

Aucuba japonica (spotted laurel) is a familiar shrub with useful yellow-green splashed leaves of oval shape.

Flowers

These can be bought from a florist and so it is more important, if you are short of space, to concentrate on foliage. If you have room there are flowers that are useful and cannot be bought which may be used to fill in spaces and make your florist's flowers go further.

Sedum spectabile 'Autumn Joy' is a perennial with green leaves and flowers with a rough texture that start green in early summer, gradually turning to pink in late summer and then to dark red. They are useful at all stages and are especially long-lasting in arrangements.

Achillea filipendulina 'Corporation Gold' is a perennial with flat rough-textured gold flowers that can be cut in August when mature and hung up to dry. They are excellent as dried flowers and very strong. Plant them from October to March in sun or partial shade.

Euphorbia polychroma is a perennial with yellow-green flowers in spring that last a long time on the plant and in water. Plant from September to October in full sun.

Eryngium (sea holly) is a perennial with blue flowers that dry well. Plant from October to April in full sun and cut for drying in August. *E. alpinum*, *E. oliverianum*, *E. maritimum* and *E. giganteum* (dies after flowering) are useful for flower arrangements.

Hydrangea is a shrub with invaluable flowers for use in autumn and for drying in winter. Plant from October to April in a sheltered position against a wall or hedge or under trees.

Allium is a bulbous plant with flowers in a ball shape. They can be dried if cut and hung up in June. Plant in sun from September to October under soil three times the depth of the bulb. Leave in the ground and do not lift for winter. Good species include *A. rosenbachianum*, *A. porrum* (leek), *A. albopilosum*.

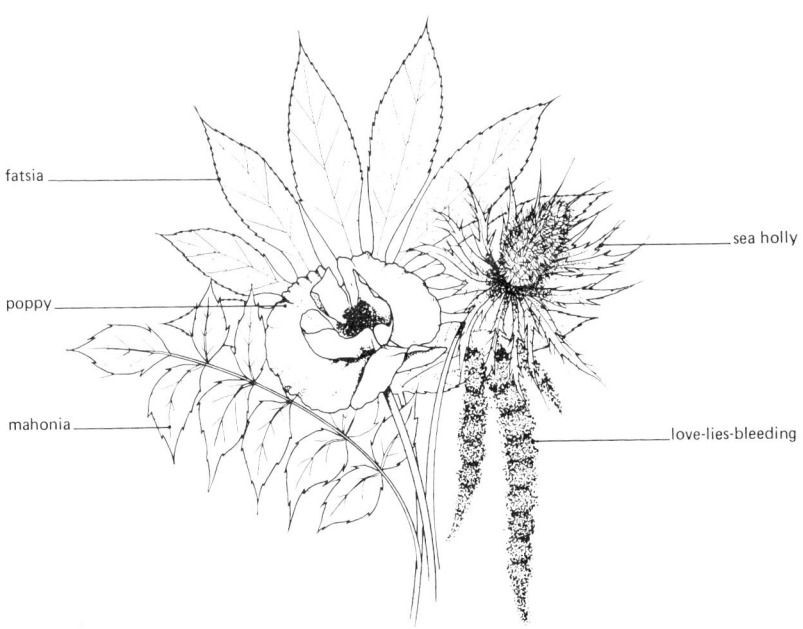

Annual flowers for drying

Some seeds produce plants that live for one year only and are called annuals. There are many of these but a useful group is one with flowers that dry easily for winter arrangements. Some seed catalogues offer collections. Follow the planting instructions on the packet in which you buy the seed. The following are useful:

Helipterum roseum which has small pink and white flowers
Helichrysum, the everlasting or straw flower in many colours
Amaranthus caudatus (love-lies-bleeding) in green and red trails
Nigella damascena (love-in-a-mist) with blue and white flowers
Papaver somniferum (opium poppy) with good seedheads
Cut the flowers or seedheads in late summer and hang them up to dry in a place that is not damp.

Bedding-out plants

Nurserymen and market stalls have bedding-out plants in early summer. These are small plants grown from seed to save you the trouble. They flower through the summer and then you discard them. Geraniums are a good buy because their leaves are useful for flower arrangements. Others that have flowers for the summer are *Calendula* (English marigold), *Dianthus barbatus* (Sweet William which lasts two years and the flowers appear in the second year), *Zinnia elegans* (exotic Mexican flowers), *Nicotiana affinis* (tobacco plant with small flowers in many colours on long stems), *Antirrhinum* (snapdragon with tall flowers) and *Matthiola* (annual stock).

Buying seeds and plants

The plants suggested will give you a basic collection of flowers and leaves with a variety of colours, shapes and sizes. You can then continue to add others when you see anything you like. Seeds are relatively inexpensive to buy and mistakes do not matter much but plants, especially shrubs, are expensive and so careful buying is important. They can be obtained from local nurseries or through orders to reputable growers. It is cheaper to buy locally because carriage and packing is added if plants are sent to you. Another advantage of buying locally is that you are more likely to find plants that suit the part of the country in which you live. The nurseryman will also give advice on planting and the position in which the plant will thrive. A lot of growing time and money can be wasted on plants that prove useless for flower arrangements, or are not suitable for your soil or the climate of your garden.

It is fun to browse over plant and seed catalogues. However it is better not to rely on the brief description of the plants unless you are experienced otherwise you may find the results when grown are not what you expected. It is preferable to see the growing plant before buying one for yourself, or at least to take advice from experienced flower arrangers and gardeners, or gardening and flower arrangement journals. Many country houses that are open to the public have extensive gardens containing labelled plants and you can copy down the names of those you like. The Royal Horticultural Society has gardens at Wisley in Surrey and The Royal National Rose Society has rose gardens at St Albans. Both these are well worth a visit for the purpose of selecting plants. Parks and garden centres also have established plants that are often labelled with their names. Your own friends may have interesting plants in their gardens and be willing to give you a clump of something you like, when dividing in autumn or early spring. Visits to horticultural and flower arrangement shows are extremely helpful and you will see the latest varieties as well as established plants. When you are there ask the nurserymen questions, see how the flower arrangers have used the flowers and foliage, and take the opportunity to buy plants and useful accessories. Local papers advertise these shows.

Plant names

The botanical names of plants may seem complicated and confusing to you. They may also be difficult to pronounce but do not be afraid of this because even the experts disagree on the pronunciation. You may find it easier to write down the name accurately and hand it to a nurseryman. It is necessary for botanical names to be used as popular, or common names, are not reliable. Unlike the botanical names they vary in different parts of the country and you may get the wrong plant when you order. You will gradually learn the correct names as you work with plants.

Preserving

Preserved leaves are invaluable for arrangements. They can be combined with fresh or dried flowers or used alone. People without gardens find they are useful to add to an arrangement of florist's flowers. They are also practical in centrally heated rooms if you want especially long-lasting arrangements. Semi-permanent designs can be made with preserved leaves arranged in a container and fresh flowers added from time to time.

Preserving with glycerine

The method of preserving leaves is very simple and involves exchanging the water in the leaves and stems for glycerine. This keeps the shape of the plant material and there is no shrivelling. The leaves remain supple and last for years. The colour changes from green to various shades of brown, ranging from cream to chocolate, according to the type of plant. Most people prefer green leaves in summer but when foliage is scarce or in bad condition during winter, preserved leaves are an excellent substitute. Very few flowers and only some leaves can be preserved. Try first with beech leaves in July or August.

Method   Buy a small bottle of glycerine from a chemist.

Pick three or four branches of beech leaves about one and a half to three feet long.

Trim away damaged leaves and any that seem to be crowding others.

Scrape off about two inches (5 cm) of outside bark on the stem end, with a kitchen knife.

Split about two inches (5 cm) of the stem, using flower scissors.

Pour the glycerine into a jar or jug and then fill the empty bottle twice over with hot water. Always use twice as much water as glycerine.

Stir the solution well to mix it otherwise the glycerine sinks to the bottom and cannot be taken up by the stem-end.

The reason for mixing the glycerine with water is that it is too thick to be taken up by the stem unless it is diluted.

Place the stem end in the warm glycerine and water solution and keep the jar in a cool, dry place until the leaves have all turned a different colour. Beech takes about a week.

If the solution is used up before the leaves have turned colour add some more to the jar.

When you remove the preserved branches from the solution, mop

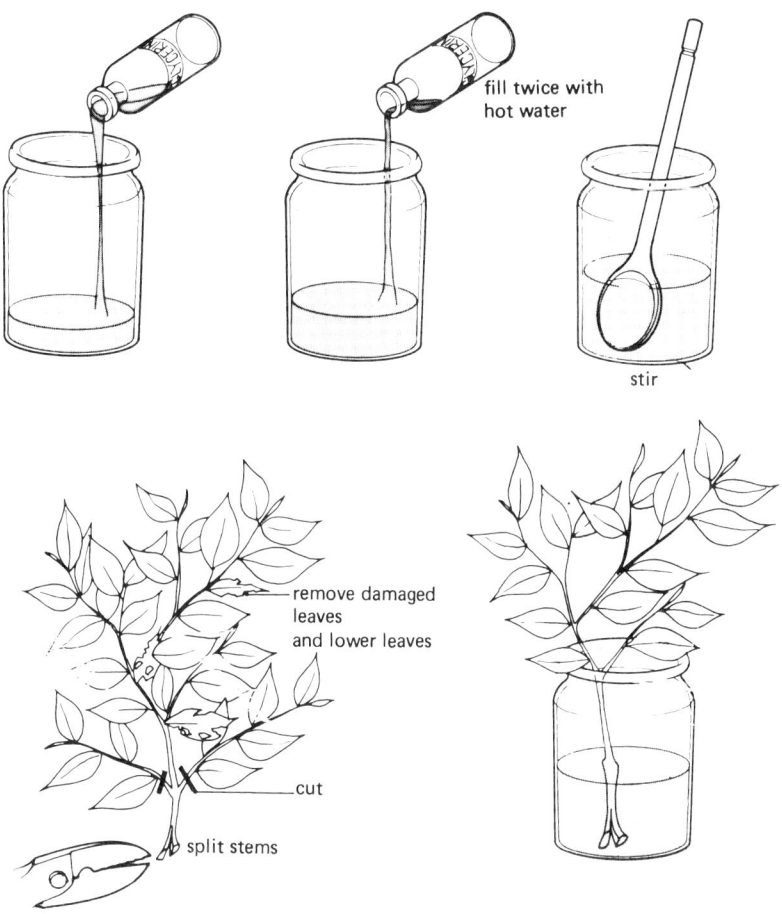

fill twice with
hot water

stir

remove damaged
leaves
and lower leaves

cut

split stems

the stem ends with a tissue so they do not drip. Store the branches in a dry place such as a cardboard box or place them in a vase or jar, without water. You can also arrange them straight away to enjoy in your home. Never store preserved leaves in a polythene bag as they can become mildewed. Beech leaves may only last a year if used continually in a hot room but there are other leaves that last indefinitely. The glycerine and water solution can be used again until it is all taken up. It is helpful to warm it before the stem ends are placed into it as a warm solution travels more quickly up the stems.

Try preserving branches of oak, sweet chestnut, *Mahonia*, Solomon's seal, *Eucalyptus* (the florist sells it during autumn and winter), rose, *Fatsia japonica* or box. Experiment with the leaves of other plants. Some may shrivel but the glycerine is not wasted if the stems do not take it up.

The brown colourings of preserved leaves look lovely with fresh flowers and you can lighten the shade by standing the preserved leaves in full sun for a few days. After arranging the leaves in water or foam with fresh flowers, mop the stem ends with a tissue when you remove them from the container to avoid mildew. Store in a dry place when not being used.

Preserving by drying

Seedheads and some flowers dry well and can be used for winter arrangements. Leaves do not dry successfully: they lose their shape and become shrivelled. They are better preserved by the glycerine method. Dried flowers cannot be used in water or wet foam as they absorb it and become soft and mildewed. Use dry foam instead.

Flowers and seedheads with strong rigid stems are normally the ones that dry well. Many dry naturally on the plant when it is growing out-of-doors but are prone to weather damage and so it is better to dry them in the house. Cut the stems as long as possible and pull or cut off the leaves because these shrivel. Bunch the stems but if the flowers crowd each other space them out by pulling the stems to different lengths. Place an elastic band several times around the end of the stems and hang the flowers upside-down so that drooping stems are avoided. It is a good idea to hang them from a wire coat hanger. Put them in a dry dark place such as the airing cupboard. As soon as they feel papery, probably in three or four days, they are dry and should be removed. Store them in cardboard boxes, stand them in jars of dry sand or hang them in bunches in a dry place. You can also arrange them straight away in dry foam in a container.

The original colour of the flowers is always lost slightly but drying and storing in a dark place tends to lessen this fading. An arrangement of dried flowers is therefore better positioned out of strong light.

Try drying grasses, pussy willow and bulrushes from the countryside, delphiniums and larkspurs from the florist (from June to August), *Achillea* flowers and honesty and *Allium* seedheads from the garden. Hydrangeas dry well in September and October. Pick the flowers when they feel slightly papery in the centre and place the stem-ends in about an inch of water, allowing the flowers to dry slowly. Try drying other flowers and seedheads from the garden and countryside, looking for those with strong stems.

Wiring dried flowers   If you have grown annual flowers for drying they may need a false stem made of wire as their own stems tend to shrivel. Special wire can be obtained from a florist. Ask for stub wires gauge 20 or 22 and mention the purpose for which they are needed. The flowers are better wired before they dry because it is difficult to push wire into a dried flower. Cut a flower from its stem and push a stub wire through the centre of the flower, until it disappears. Alternatively you can push a wire up through the base of the flower into the centre. The flower closes on the wire as it dries. The wire making this false stem can be hidden by placing it into a section of

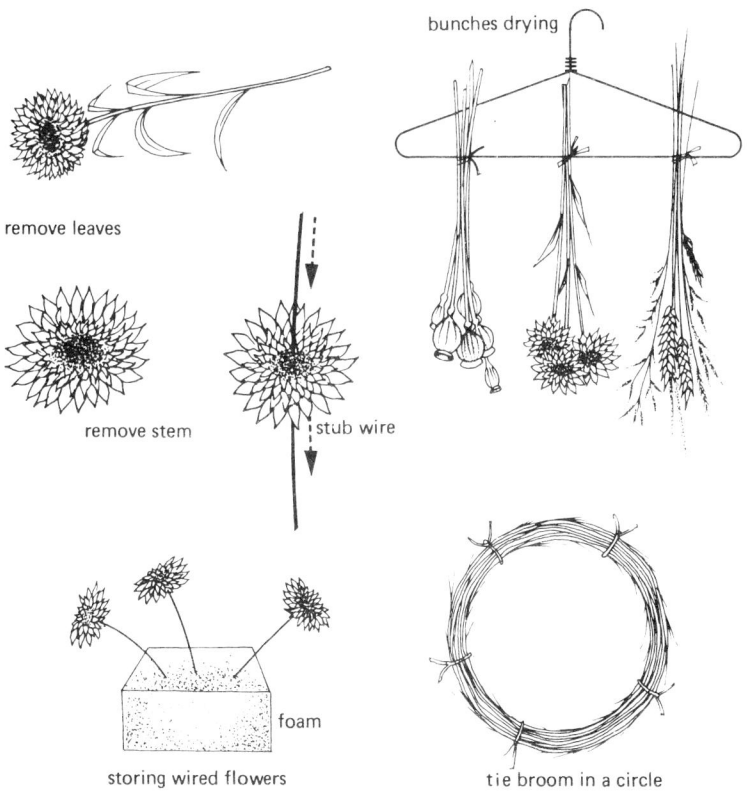

remove leaves

bunches drying

remove stem

stub wire

storing wired flowers

foam

tie broom in a circle

hollow stem. (Grasses often have hollow stems.) Arrange the flowers at once or store by pushing the wires into a block of dry foam.

Drying fruit and vegetables   Gourds, artichokes and pomegranates from the greengrocer can be dried in an airing cupboard. Leave them in the bottom of the cupboard until they seem light in weight. Artichokes take a few days and look dramatic when sprayed with gold paint for Christmas arrangements. Gourds and pomegranates may take several weeks and become lighter in colour but they can last indefinitely. They can be grouped in a bowl with fresh fruit.

Broom   Broom grows wild in Scotland and many people have it in their gardens. This can be dried into swirls for arrangements. Cut a two-foot length with a thin stem. Thick stems will not bend easily. Tie the stem into a circle, using string or wool, in several places. More than one piece of broom can be tied together. If you have a lampshade ring it is easy to tie the broom on to this in a circular shape. Place it in the airing cupboard to dry for a few days and then cut the string. The broom should remain in curves. These can be sprayed with gold, copper or silver paint for Christmas arrangements.

Things to collect

Driftwood

The term driftwood refers to any pieces of wood that have been weathered by the elements and not only to wood that has been in water before being tossed back on land. Driftwood can be found in places where there are trees and the best time to look is after storms. Branches, chunks of roots, tree-trunks and bark can be found on beaches, lakeshores, woodlands and places where land is being cleared for building.

It is unusual to find a piece that is perfect in shape, hardness, colour and cleanliness. Most wood needs some treatment before it is fit to use with flowers in the house. However it is well worth a little effort because it lasts for ever. No piece is the same as another and so your wood will be unique and stimulate a lot of interest.

Look for hard wood or pieces that have few rotting parts. This is essential because if a large part of the wood is rotten it will break and crumble, apart from being unpleasant to have in your house. Before taking it home decide if you like the shape, or if it can be adapted, because pieces can be removed if necessary. If it is dirty it can be cleaned and the colour can be improved if it is not to your liking.

Cleaning   The first job is to clean the wood you have carried home. Grey wood should only be wiped with a damp cloth. The grey colour, caused by the sun which bleaches wood, is only on the surface and vigorous cleaning removes it. Other wood should be immersed, in a sink of warm, soapy water and given a good scrub with a brush. If there are many insects on the wood it may be necessary to spray it with insecticide before washing. Leave the piece outside for a few days until all the animal life has disappeared.

After washing let the wood dry for a few days and then, using a small pointed knife, lift away all the soft wood in crevices. Finally brush it hard with a wire hearth brush, obtainable from an ironmonger. This job is better done out-of-doors or in an outhouse as it causes a lot of dust.

The wood should now be in good condition. Look at it from various angles to decide if any superfluous pieces need sawing or clipping off. Sometimes a chunk of wood will stand on its own successfully if a small piece is removed. It is better not to do this unless really necessary because it leaves a raw scar.

Colour   Most wood has an attractive natural colour and is better left unchanged. A coat of clear wax gives a soft sheen and some protection from water. Rub in plenty of colourless shoe or furniture polish and leave it overnight before polishing with a brush or cloth. If you wish to change the colour use shoe polish containing light or dark brown stain. Try the polish on a part of the wood that does not show first to see if you like it. It is also possible to varnish and paint driftwood but this tends to give an unnatural appearance that may not be attractive with flowers. Mat polyurethane polish protects the wood without making it shiny.

Support in a design   Small pieces of wood and bark can be placed in front of a pinholder or foam block to hide it. They lean against the mechanics and need no further means of support. Larger chunks stand alone and can be used on a base. A food tin, containing a pinholder or block of foam, can be placed behind the wood to hold flowers and leaves. If it does not stand exactly in the position in which you want it, a small chunk of wood, a lump of plasticine or some other sort of wedge, may be used to hold it in place. It may be worthwhile to nail a small piece of wood on to the chunk as a permanent prop.

Lightweight branches can be inserted into plastic foam or on to a pinholder if the bottom of the branch is split in several places. Often there is a length of branch that can be rested on the inside of a container for support, so that the main branch hangs down the side. False legs can be added by means of thin wooden rods called dowels bought from a Do-it-yourself shop. Make a hole one inch deep in the driftwood using a drill of the same diameter as the dowel. Make sure that the hole is at the correct angle for the dowel so that support is given to the wood in the desired place. Push the dowel into the hole and cut it to a suitable length. Sometimes it is worth asking a carpenter to do this for you.

Crosscuts   A crosswise cutting of a tree-trunk makes a useful base. If you come across men felling trees with a saw you may find them willing to cut off a two-inch deep crosscut for you. Sandpaper the wood and then varnish it for protection with mat polyurethane varnish.

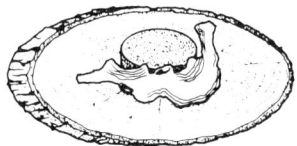

driftwood hides mechanics

crosscut for a base

Pine and fir cones

These may be collected where there are cone-bearing trees. They need no special treatment, but if they are wet, a few days in a warm dry place will make them open out. They give an attractive rough texture in winter designs of evergreens and can be sprayed with gold, silver and copper paint for use at Christmas. A false stem of wire can be added to support a cone in an arrangement. Use two long stubwires, gauge 20 or 22, bought from a florist, for each cone. Tuck the middle of one wire into the lower scales of the cone near the point where it has been joined to the tree. Do the same thing on the opposite side with the other wire so that the two wires are

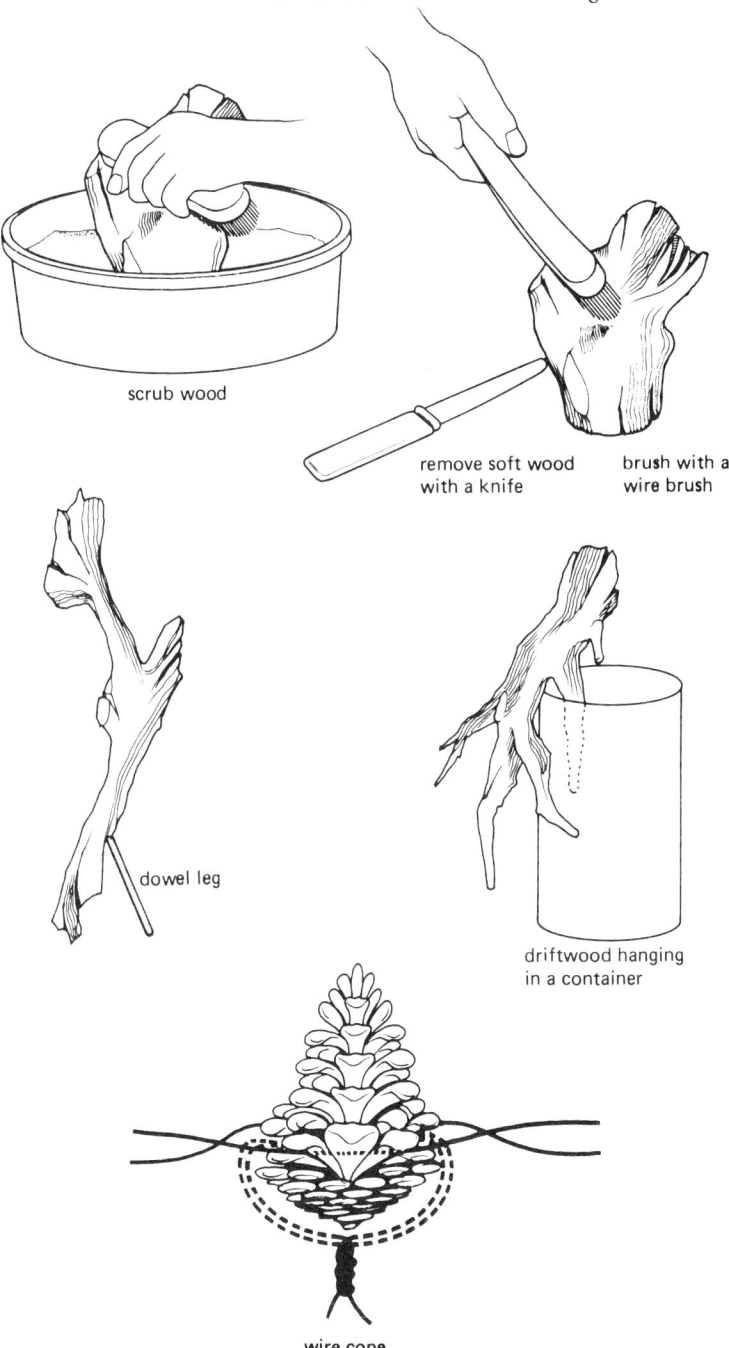

scrub wood

remove soft wood
with a knife

brush with a
wire brush

dowel leg

driftwood hanging
in a container

wire cone

Dried bulrushes combined with fresh irises, laurel leaves and twigs on a pinholder in a food tin concealed by a chunk of driftwood. The base is a crosscut of a tree-trunk.

Three chrysanthemums arranged simply on a pinholder in a glass bowl with a twist of wood and two leaves. Broken windscreen glass conceals the pinholder.

parallel, either side of the central core of the cone. Twist the wires together on both sides of the cone and then bend them down below the base of the cone. Twist all four ends together to form a false stem. Several cones can be wired into a cluster.

Stones

Apart from washing, nothing need be done to stones. Some people own polishing machines which give them an attractive sheen, but rough ones are just as attractive with flowers. It is usually better to collect three or four flat stones of the same type and colour, varying in size from two to four inches (5–10 cm) long. It is then easy to group them around a pinholder to hide it.

Broken windscreen glass

Broken windscreen glass can often be found in a lay-by. Gather it up with care into a bag. It is not usually sharp but you may prefer to pick it up with gloves on. A pile of this glass covers a pinholder well and looks pretty under water especially in a glass container.

Stone and slate for bases

Look for pieces of stone and slate about half an inch thick. Lengths of about twelve inches (30 cm) are useful and they should be flat, otherwise containers do not stand firmly on them. The cream, blue-grey and green colourings are good with the colours of flowers. Pieces can be found in mining districts and in mountainous country. To avoid scratching polished furniture, stick a piece of felt on the underside using a clear adhesive.

Things to make

Bases

You can make bases with pieces of wood that can be covered with fabric, such as velvet or linen. A cakeboard from a stationer's shop can also be covered. Buy a circle of wood, between ten and fourteen inches (25–30 cm) in diameter and about a quarter to half an inch (1 cm) thick, from a Do-it-yourself shop. Cut a piece of fabric about three inches (8 cm) wider all the way round and tack down a quarter inch (1 cm) turning round the edge. Turn the fabric over again to give a three-quarter inch (2 cm) tube and tack this down. Machine or sew by hand using a small running stitch. Leave a one-inch (2·5 cm) opening for threading in a length of elastic. Use a safety pin for slotting in the elastic. Tighten it so that the fabric is gathered up and tie the ends together, cutting off any spare elastic. Place the cover on the board. It can be removed for washing or when you want a change of colour or texture. Sludgy-looking green, brown, beige, navy and other dull colours are better to use than brilliant ones which compete with the flowers.

Containers

1 *A large, round meat can*   Ask your butcher to save you an empty cooked meat can with one end left on so that it will hold water. The outside of the can may be made more attractive by covering it in different ways:

i a straw mat cut to fit and glued on with clear adhesive

ii self-adhesive fabric or paper (linen or Fablon) cut one inch (2·5 cm) longer than the can at each end. Clip the ends down for one inch (2·5 cm) in several places to make a neat turn. Fold over the top into the tin and the bottom on to the base of the tin. If the edges look uneven a length of braid can be gluded around the top and the bottom of the can

iii paint the can with emulsion or green blackboard paint which both have a mat texture. If a handful or two of sand is added to the paint it will dry with a slightly rough surface.

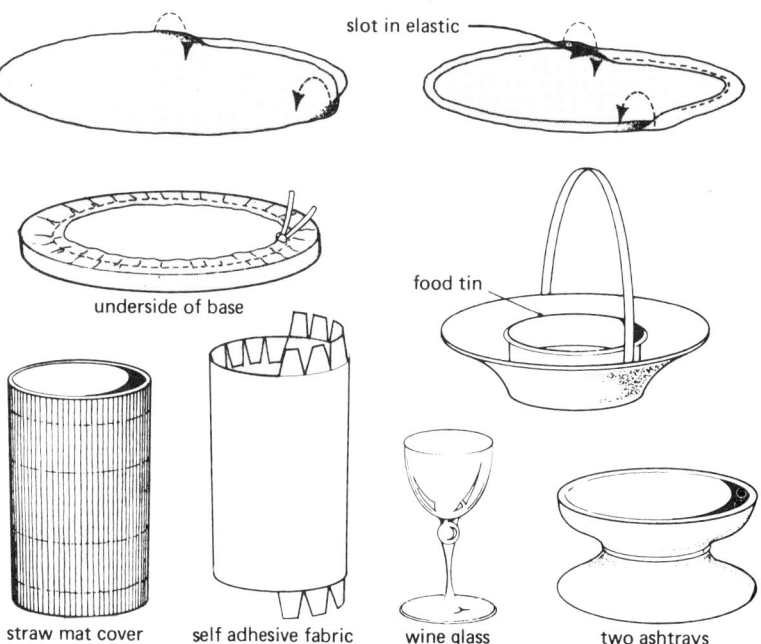

slot in elastic

underside of base

food tin

straw mat cover   self adhesive fabric   wine glass   two ashtrays

2 *A basket or wooden box*   Containers that do not hold water can be used for flowers if you place an empty food tin inside to hold water and mechanics.

3 *Ashtrays*   Two heavy glass ashtrays can be glued together with clear adhesive to make a container. Choose similar shapes but one can be smaller than the other.

4 *A wine glass*   This makes a useful small container. To prevent untidy stems from being seen through the clear glass, swill paint around the inside, or paint the outside. A wine bottle can be similarly painted inside.

4. Designing with Flowers and Leaves

Once you have a small stock of materials, and have become accustomed to supporting stems in containers you will probably feel ready to find out more about designing with plant material.

The word 'designing' may suggest something complicated but it simply means 'putting in order', and this is something most people do at some time every day with a variety of objects. When you look at a jumbled heap of things your instinct is to tidy them and get some order out of the chaos. You go a step further if in addition to tidying up objects you also attempt to display them well or arrange them pleasingly. Designing flowers is simply placing them in an orderly manner and at the same time arranging them to look attractive.

The first step in designing is choosing. You select certain objects to place together. If, for example, you are giving coffee to a friend, you choose from your china cupboard suitable cups, saucers, cream jug and sugar bowl for serving coffee. In addition you probably select pieces of china that look nice together and seem related, perhaps in colour, pattern and texture. You then set them all on a tray.

In the same way instead of merely buying any bunch of flowers, you can deliberately select flowers from the ones on sale or from those growing in the garden, that suit the setting in which you are going to place them and each other. This is when designing begins.

Features to consider

The flowers should be related in size to their eventual setting. For example a large room containing heavy furniture needs big flowers but a coffee table may only have room for a small arrangement. Your first thought then should be of the size of flower to buy.

The colour of the surroundings should also influence your choice of flowers. For example orange dahlias will not show up against orange wallpaper and yellow could look better; white flowers will be lost on a white tablecloth and pink ones could be more suitable. Some colours recede and are not effective in the dim lighting of a dark hall or a candlelight supper. It is helpful to bear in mind the intended setting when choosing the colour of flowers.

There are various shapes in plant material including round flowers, long leaves, thin branches and so on. Small, round flowers may be the best choice for the centre of a dining table but tall branches may be better in the corner of a room against a high wall.

Plant material includes beautiful textures: velvety, downy, shiny and silky surfaces. A design is more interesting if both rough and smooth textures are used.

Size, colour, shape and texture are important. This is true whether you are arranging flowers, choosing furniture, displaying objects in a shop window or doing anything else that involves assembling a number of objects together. An awareness of these qualities, present in all objects, helps you to understand them whatever the medium you use.

Size

All objects have a size. When you look at a group of similar objects some appear small and others big but they look small or big only in comparison with each other and not when seen alone.

This flower is neither small nor big until it is seen next to another flower,

here it looks big.

here it looks small.

Dissimilar objects can also look small or big in comparison with each other.

a tiny cup and
a huge teapot

a big flower and a small leaf

a big leaf and a small flower

When there is a large difference between the sizes of objects seen together the bigger one can seem enormous and the smaller one tiny. We feel happier when we look at a group of objects if their sizes are closely related.

A flower arrangement is a grouping of objects and includes flowers, leaves and a container. The arrangement is more pleasing to look at if the sizes of the objects are relatively close or *in scale*.

The leaf is too big for the
container and the flower.

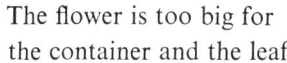

The flower is too big for
the container and the leaf.

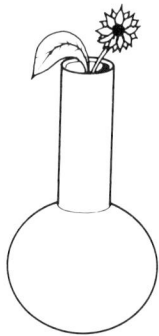

The container is too big
for the leaf and the flower.

Here the leaf, flower and container
are in scale with each other.

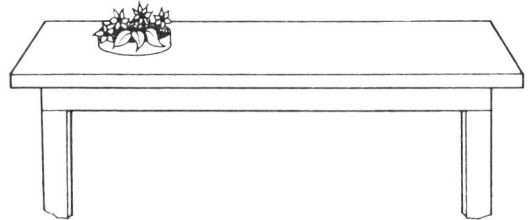

Scale is also concerned when you see a flower arrangement in its setting. A small design, about six inches (15 cm) tall, is dwarfed if it is seen on a refectory table eight feet (2·4 m) long.

A three-foot (91 cm) tall flower arrangement is too big for a hospital bedside table.

'Too big' and 'too small' relate to individual objects in a grouping and also to the whole grouping in its setting:

Look at:

a tree that is too big for a small garden

a small woman in a large hat

a small painting on a large wall

Try:

an arrangement using large leaves and small flowers (or the other way round)

picking a bunch of leaves in several sizes and finding out which is
the most suitable size for each of your containers
an arrangement in a thimble
an arrangement in a large basket

Colour

It is fortunate that our choice of colour is more limited when
buying flowers than it is when selecting paint or fabric colours. This
is because the florist cannot have many different flowers at one time
and the colours of your room also restrict the choice and provide
a guideline.

You may decide to echo the colours of a cushion or a lampshade
in your room, to match the curtains or to have an exciting contrast.
When the flowers are placed near to a painting you may like to select
one of the colours from it for the flowers so that the picture and the
arrangement are in harmony.

It is dull to buy the same colour each time for your room and it
is a challenge to try different colour combinations each time you
make an arrangement.

The use of one colour

It is almost impossible to make an arrangement of only one colour
with plant material. This is because flowers usually have green stems
and sometimes yellow centres, whatever the colour of the petals.
Many flowers and leaves also have variegated colouring. The nearest
to a one-coloured design is an arrangement of foliage in greens.
Normally it is a matter of one dominating colour. This can give
a dramatic effect and can look pleasing in a room in which there
are already many colours.

Colour variation

Broadly speaking colours fall into six groups or families: yellow,
orange, red, violet, blue and green. However within each group
there are many variations of each colour or hue. Think of all the
names that are given to different shades of red; cerise, pink, pillar-
box, magenta, maroon, raspberry, strawberry, cherry, wine, claret,
ruby, crimson, brick, russet, burgundy and so on. Each one is a
variation of red but is within the same family. For this reason all

An arrangement of leaves of varying shapes and shades of green. No base is used because the container looks heavy and large.

the variations of a hue usually look attractive together. In fact, an arrangement of red flowers often looks better if a number of reds are included. You can combine carnations in several reds, or red dahlias, roses and gladioli in slightly different shades.

Variations of colour are beautiful and we should take advantage of them. As an experiment take a look in your garden or a park and count the number of greens you can see. There may be blue-greens, yellow-greens and grey-greens, dark and light greens, brilliant and dull greens, shiny and mat greens, variegated and plain greens. Using a variety of a hue in an arrangement seems to add life and interest to it.

Combining colours

Green safely combines with all colours, perhaps because it is often seen with other colours in nature. There are no rules for other colour combinations and it is interesting to try colours that you have not thought of mixing before, such as yellow and pink, blue and orange, violet and yellow, blue and mauve, orange and cerise, brown and grey.

Our eyes normally look for a relationship between colours. It is easy to see that yellow, orange and red are related if you do a small experiment with paint. Borrow a child's water-colour paintbox and mix a pool of yellow paint. Add a little red paint to this and the result will be orange. Do the same with a pool of blue paint, adding red, and the result is violet. Blue added to yellow will produce green. These groups of colours: yellow, orange, red; blue, violet, red; blue, green and yellow go happily together and are sometimes called adjacent colours.

Dark and light colours   If you add white paint to one of the colours you have mixed it becomes lighter and is called a *tint*. If you add black to one of the colours it becomes darker and is called a *shade*. If both white and black are added the result is a greyed version of the original colour and this is called a *tone*.

When combining flowers in different colours the following guidelines are helpful:

1 *Repetition* of a colour helps to give unity. An isolated spot of colour attracts the eye too much and 'a mate' in the same colour looks better. One white flower for example in a group of pink ones

looks lonely and the addition of a few more white flowers will help the design.

2 *Different weights* of colour in all those combined are interesting. Dark colours look heavy and light ones appear to have less weight. Maroon, deep violet and navy blue are heavy in appearance while pale pink, cream and apricot look lighter. If different weights of colour are used together the design has more life. For example dark red roses with dark green holly leaves can look heavy and lifeless and may be improved with the addition of variegated yellow and green holly.

3 *Many brilliant colours combined* together can look restless and be tiring to the eyes. It is better to use soft colours when you are using many in one arrangement. The Dutch and Flemish flower painters combined colours with superb skill and you can study their work in art galleries, books and on greetings cards. Most of them show repetition of colours and the use of soft not brilliant colours in varying weights.

4 *White* does not combine well with every colour as one might suppose. It seems to be unrelated, for example, to deep red or violet. It seems less far apart from lighter colours such as yellow, pink and pale blue.

5 *The amount of each colour* you use changes the appearance of a design. There are no rules and a lot depends on the range of colours you choose. Most people prefer to look at smaller quantities of brilliant colours and larger areas of paler or duller colours.

Warm and cool colours

Orange and red are warm colours and blue and green are cool colours. Yellow and violet look warm or cool depending on the colours that they are combined with. For example, when yellow is placed with red and orange it looks warmer than when it is used with blue and green. Warm colours are effective on a cool day and in rooms that are cold. Cool colours are pleasing on a hot day.

Surroundings

It is difficult to isolate colours from their surroundings. Neighbouring colours have a strong influence so that a colour seems to alter in appearance when seen against different backgrounds. Try holding lengths of different coloured fabric, or coloured card or paper, behind an arrangement to see the effect. For example, pale pink flowers look much lighter against a dark wall than against a pale coloured wall. Orange looks vibrant against blue but dull in front of yellow. The way colour can change its appearance in different surroundings is one of its most fascinating qualities.

Lighting

The colours in a room also change according to the amount and type of light. The time of the day, the season, the amount of sunshine, the type of artificial lighting, all make a difference, so that colours are constantly changing in a room. There are some helpful guidelines:

1 Flowers placed with the main light behind them will lose colour. They look brighter when light falls directly on to them.

2 Candlelight is so dim that only the lightest colours such as white, yellow, apricot, pink, cream, pale mauve and pale blue can be seen. Darker colours disappear, especially violet and blue.

3 All types of electric lighting reduce the brilliance of flower colours and some lighting changes colours. The ordinary household bulb is better for reds, oranges and yellows than it is for blues, violets and greens. A white fluorescent tube yellows colours and makes red look muddy and brown, oranges look yellower, blues look greener, greens become yellow-green. Yellow is the only colour that remains true. A warm white fluorescent tube is a better buy because it adds a slightly rosy glow to colours. Reds and oranges are more pleasing, blues tend to appear more mauve, yellows and greens are warmer looking.

4 Some colours are more luminous than others and show up better in dim lighting. You can see this in a garden at sunset. White is by far the most luminous and then yellow and the tints that contain white. Yellow-green and yellow-orange are also luminous because they contain yellow. Dark blues, violets, blue-reds and blue-greens have low luminosity.

Colour movement

Colours do not actually move but they can appear to do so. Green is the only colour that does not 'move'. Reds and oranges tend to move towards you and violets and blues move away. This means that in a large room reds and oranges will seem closer to you than blues and violets. Yellow is suitable for a room with high ceilings as it is a 'lifting' colour. Dark colours with black in them are heavy looking and move downwards.

Container colours

When you make an arrangement it is normally the flowers that you are displaying rather than the container, which is a receptacle for holding water and the flower stems. If the container is seen, it should be attractive because it is part of the whole design, but it should not compete with the flowers and should be chosen to show them up well.

When you buy a new container it is sensible to choose one that will harmonize with all the colours in flowers. For example, a brilliant scarlet container can look exciting with an arrangement of all reds but otherwise its use is limited because yellow, blue and violet may not blend well with the scarlet. There are many black and white containers, sold specifically for flowers, but these are not as useful as one would expect. White is a strong colour that attracts attention away from the flowers. Black tends to look heavy.

Flowers in a garden are seen against a background of browns and greens. These colours appear harmonious with any colour of flower. Present-day cooking dishes and bowls are often made in shades of brown and they can be used for flower arranging as well as cooking. Craftsmen potters make stoneware containers in perfect colourings for arrangements. All neutralized colours (those with little colour in them) are sympathetic with flower colours and do not vie with them for attention. If you remember the colours of the earth when buying a container you are unlikely to go wrong.

Natural colour schemes

Combinations of colours can be called colour schemes or colour harmonies. There are many ideas for colour schemes in the world around us. Once you begin to be really aware of them you will find it fascinating to look out for them. For example, flowers themselves often show more than one colour, especially pansies, hydrangeas, tulips. Then there are birds with lovely colourings such as tits, chaffinches and peacocks. Butterflies, shells, stones and jewels all have beautiful colourings. Stormy days, brilliant sunsets, misty mornings and woodlands, cornfields and seashores can give inspiration. The paintings of good artists are excellent for study, not only for their colour schemes but for the amount of each colour they use.

The personality of colour

Colour has the power of being very expressive and can easily establish an atmosphere. It can make a room, or a flower arrangement in the room, look pretty, dull, quiet, dramatic, rich, drab, gay, soft, harsh, brilliant and so on. This is often because of the associations that we have with certain colours. Blue reminds us of sea and sky and gives a tranquil feeling but it can also look cold and distant. Green reminds us of lawns and woodlands although yellow-green has a more active, youthful appearance like young plant growth. Violet can be mysterious, shy and retiring, 'the modest violet', but a rich violet can be associated with splendour as it was favoured by early kings. Black can be depressing, dramatic, smart, and white may have innocence and purity but it can also be cold like snow. Grey is melancholy but can have softness and subtlety and be reminiscent of old age. Yellow reminds us of sunshine, spring-time and youth but a gold shade looks expensive. Red can be exciting, warm like a fire, angry and dangerous but it is also the colour of pageantry and carnivals. Orange tends to be autumnal but it is also warm.

The associations and personalities of colours are useful in flower arrangements for special effects. Pinks, reds and oranges look gay and are stimulating for a party. Blues and greens are quiet and restful and may be suitable to send to a patient in hospital. Yellows can bring sunshine on a dull day and tints are appropriate for a baby's christening party.

Look at:
the colour schemes other people use in their homes
the weight of different colours in a room
the colours of flowers in candlelight
the colours in a sunset, storm, flower, bird, fabric, jewel and stone
the colours used in advertisements
the paintings in a library book of an artist, such as Gauguin, Picasso, Constable, Monet, Turner. Study each artist's colour preferences, the range of colours in each painting and
the amounts of each colour used in the painting

Try:
arranging leaves in several greens with flowers of one colour
using in one design, several reds in flowers with several greens in foliage

an arrangement using the colours seen in a painting

an arrangement of leaves in any colour but not green

an arrangement echoing the colours of a shell, flower, stone, feather

playing with water-colour paint in a paint-box or with five tubes of gouache paint in black, white, red, yellow and blue. Mix a pool of one colour and add portions of white gradually. After each mix paint a slash of colour on white paper to give a range of tints. Do the same with a pool of colour and black and then with a colour and grey

cutting scraps of coloured paper from a magazine and arrange them in pleasing groups of colours

making arrangements that look rich, frugal, pretty, sunny, delicate, dramatic and brilliant because of their colouring

Shape

After considering the sizes and colours of flowers, then shape is a quality to think about. There are many different shapes and combinations of shapes in the world about us.

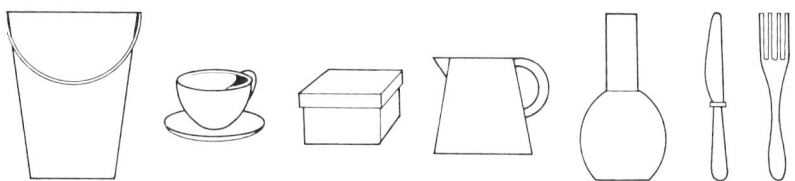

Shapes can be geometric or without definite shape, symmetrical or asymmetrical, long or short, thick or thin, curved or straight and so on.

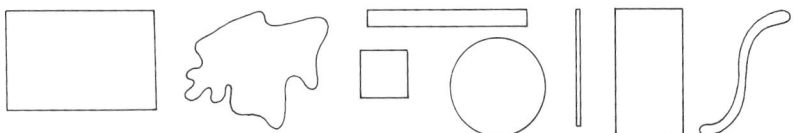

They can be two-dimensional like the drawings on this page which only have height and width or they can be three-dimensional like

a chair or an apple with height, width and depth.

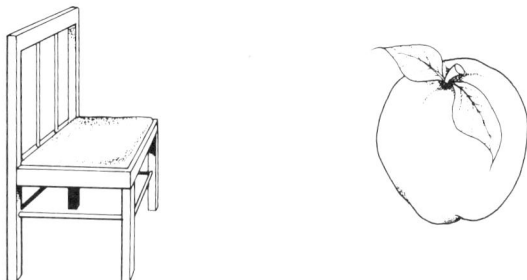

Shapes can also be solid like a block of wood or have space inside like a lampshade frame.

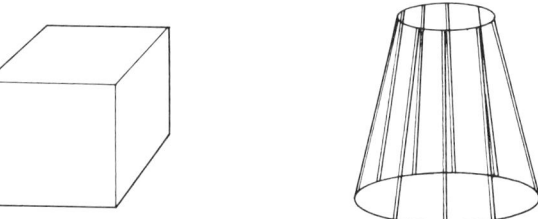

Shapes can be symmetrical, that is the same shape either side of the centre, or asymmetrical, that is different shapes either side of the centre.

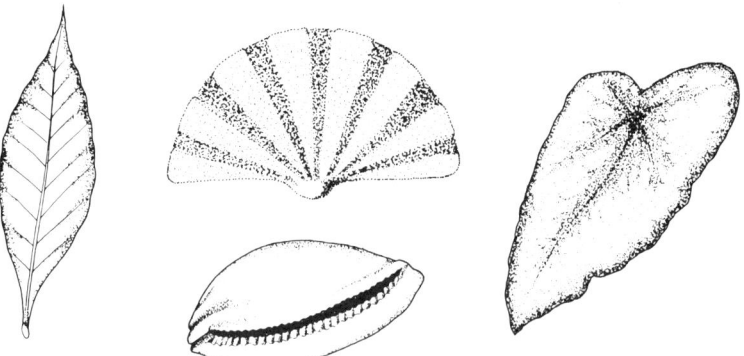

There are many shapes in plant material. Speaking generally they can be divided into three main groups – long shapes called *lines* in design terms, which move the eyes along;

round, or near round shapes called *points* in design which hold the eyes in one place;

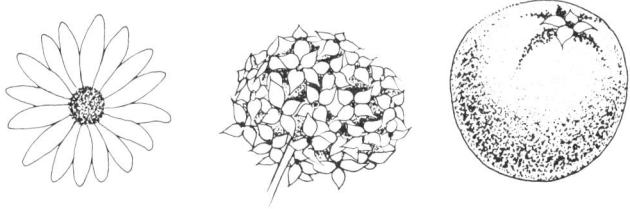

and shapes in-between these others which are neither long nor round and which are sometimes called *transitional shapes.*

A flower arrangement is made up of a number of shapes in the same way that a dress is made up from a number of pieces of fabric. When stitched together these pieces of fabric make another complete shape in the form of a dress. In a similar way the individual flowers, leaves, branches and container are assembled together to make another complete shape, in the form of a flower arrangement.

It is possible to make a design of plant material which is all similar in shape. For example it can be made of branches which are all line material. Oranges and apples grouped in a bowl make up a design of all rounds. An arrangement of foliage can be a design using all transitional shapes.

It is not possible to make an arrangement of all rounds with flowers unless you cut off the stems or hide them. If the stems show, then

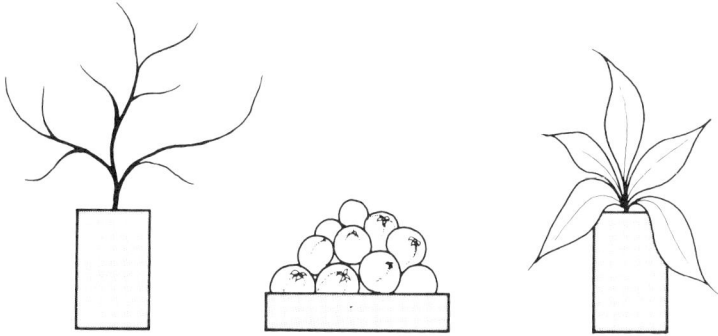

you have a design of rounds and lines. An arrangement of all round flowers can look very static and monotonous unless you turn some of the flowers to face different ways. You can also add some flowers of a different size to improve the design. Leaves in a transitional shape can soften the bare stems of the flowers. An arrangement of all lines may look restless and a few rounds added to the design gives some resting places for your eyes.

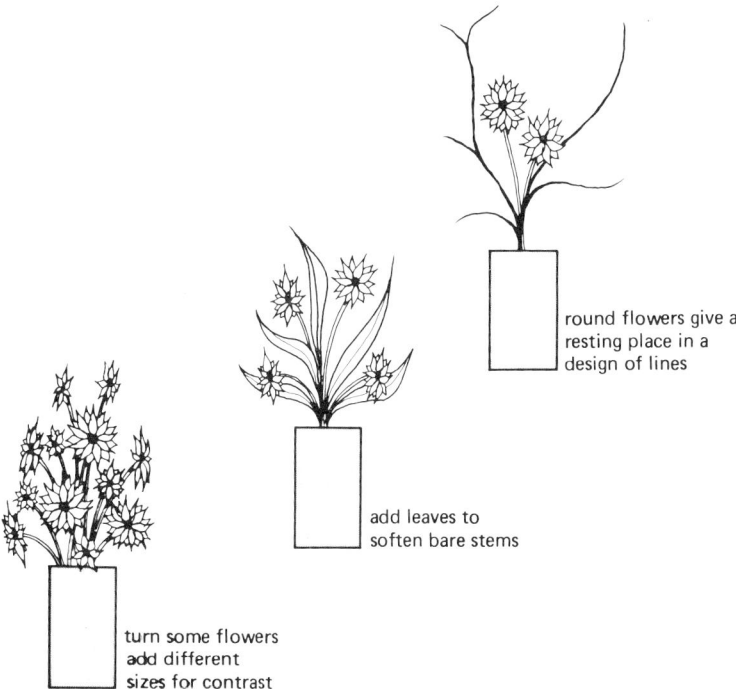

round flowers give a
resting place in a
design of lines

add leaves to
soften bare stems

turn some flowers
add different
sizes for contrast

Space

To be seen clearly, shapes require space. When you look at a heap of rubbish it is almost impossible to see the individual shapes of each object in the heap. If you wish to see an object clearly then it must be separated from the others.

A group of objects can be separated with a lot of space between them or they can be drawn close together. The amount of space you use between objects can be varied to give a different effect. When arranging flowers you may put them close together with only a little space around each one or you may place them further apart with a lot of space between each one. It depends on which style you choose.

line   mass

Experienced flower arrangers call designs that use little space within them *mass arrangements*. Those with a lot of space within the design and few pieces of plant material are called *line arrangements*. In summer when flowers are plentiful, and cost less, a mass arrangement is easy to do and you can enjoy the effect of massed colour and texture. A line design is sympathetic with the winter scene out-of-doors and is economical when flowers are expensive and foliage is scarce. This type of arrangement enables you to enjoy the beauty of individual shapes rather than the loveliness of massed colour.

When you make a line design there is no strong geometric, or regular, outline. When you mass flowers and leaves with little space between them you become more concerned with a definite outline and normally a regular, rather than an irregular, shape is more pleasing.

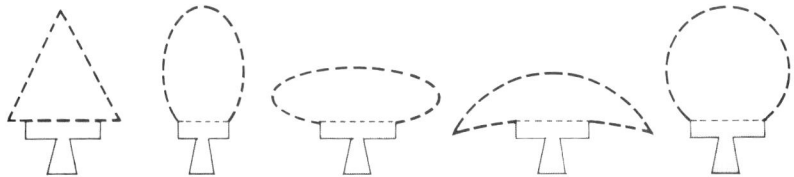

The design you make, whether it is a line or a mass arrangement, can be higher than it is wide or wider than it is high, depending on the setting and purpose of the arrangement. For example, on a dining table for a seated meal a wide, low design is more suitable than a high one.

Look at:
the way clouds change shape
the varying shapes of fruit and vegetables at the greengrocers
the way shells, stones, flowers change shape as you turn all of these
in different directions

Try:

an arrangement with a lot of open space in the centre
a design with a solid outline
an arrangement, like a fan, with regular spaces
an arrangement of irregular spaces between each piece of plant material
a low, horizontal design
a high, slim design
an arrangement of branches only, then one of round flowers, then one of leaves, finally try all three shapes together
a design using only straight stemmed plant material and then a design using only material with curved stems
an arrangement of branches or leaves framing one flower

Texture

When you have become practised in combining different shapes there is texture to consider. The surface of every object has a texture of some kind and there are many variations such as fluffy, silky, smooth, prickly, rough, knobbly, and so on.

Texture is normally a word you think of in connection with objects that you touch, such as a tweed jacket, silk curtains, a wood sculpture. Some textural surfaces are inviting to touch and others are not. You may feel like touching a fluffy rabbit but not a slimy worm.

There are many varieties of texture in plant material including velvety pansies, sticky horse-chestnut buds, downy peaches, fluffy grasses, prickly thistles or smooth leaves. Some are inviting to touch and some are not. A flower arrangement is not designed to be touched, but without touching your eyes can tell you the feel. Just by looking you know there are differences in the surfaces of the pieces of plant material.

Many things look and feel the same: for example a rose stem looks and feels prickly. A carnation flower however has a rough appearance, because its surface is broken up, but it feels silky to the touch. This kind of texture is called *visual texture* by flower arrangers who are concerned with the *textural appearance* of plant material rather than its feel.

Visual textures, broadly speaking, fall into two main groups, *rough* and *smooth*, although there are many variations of each. So in a flower arrangement the carnation is considered rough. In any design, contrasts of texture give interest and are more effective than

A basket holding scabious, daisies and sedum with leaves, supported by foam in a small tin. The sedum has been included to provide a rough-looking texture.

similarities. For example an arrangement of rough-looking, dried plant material usually looks better in a smooth pottery container than in a rough-looking basket which is too similar. Rough-looking pine cones are more effective used in front of a shiny leaf than a rough one. Rough-looking carnations look better with some plain, smooth leaves. There are many examples of contrasts of texture in nature especially in shells.

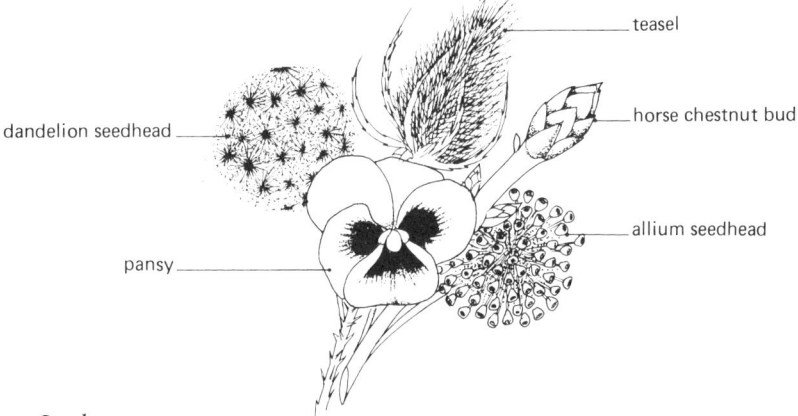

Look at:
the various textures in a room including those of the carpet, curtains, furniture and walls
a group of objects to see which look rough and which look smooth touch them to see if the look and the feel is the same
the different surface textures of fruit and vegetables in the green-grocers
the different surface textures of leaves in the garden.

Try:
an arrangement that uses a mixture of rough-looking and smooth-looking plant material
an arrangement of smooth leaves in a basket or container with a rough surface
an arrangement of rough dried plant material in a shiny container
an arrangement that includes fruit (apples can be pushed on to one end of a skewer with the other end placed in plastic foam)
a collage (or picture) of groupings of coffee beans, lentils, bird seed, dried peas, rice, small buttons, seedheads. Put a patch of clear adhesive on a sheet of cardboard and drop one group on to it. Continue doing this with other materials.

Assembling

Once you are aware of the varying sizes, colours, shapes and textures of plant material there are guidelines to learn about assembling, or *composing* them into a design. Flower arrangement is an art which involves putting together a number of units. Individual notes are put together to compose a piece of music, pieces of fabric are sewn together to make a dress, goods are assembled together in dressing a window. A flower arrangement is a *composition* of flowers, leaves, container, base and so on. All these objects are assembled to make a whole new object bearing in mind their textures, sizes, shapes and colours. As you put them together you hope that the end result will be pleasing to the eye and harmonious. It is helpful to understand some of the things that will make your arrangement a success.

Balance

If an arrangement falls over, possibly because it contains too many flowers in it for its size, then it is certainly unbalanced. Things can look unbalanced and make you feel uncomfortable even if they do not actually fall over.

The flower arrangement on the left makes you feel uneasy because all the flowers are on one side and it appears lop-sided. To look balanced it needs flowers or leaves on the other side.

The appearance of being well balanced is called *visual balance*.

Your eyes balance a flower arrangement in relation to the middle of the container and will be happier when attracted equally to both sides. This is easily achieved if you put exactly the same things either side of the centre, making the shape symmetrical. These objects are symmetrical because they possess the same shape either side of the centre.

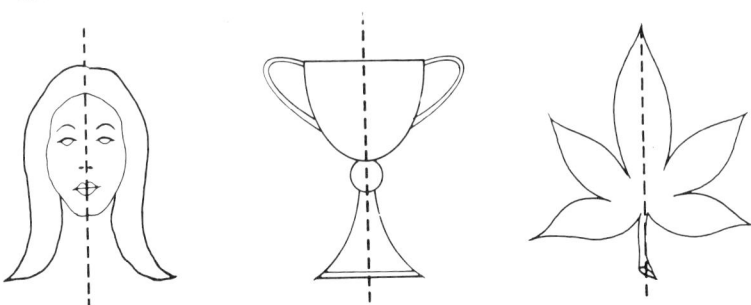

A symmetrical flower design is easily arranged. This is why a triangular shape is popular and has become a classical design in this country. A circle and an oval are also symmetrical and these two shapes have been used all through history for the arrangement of flowers.

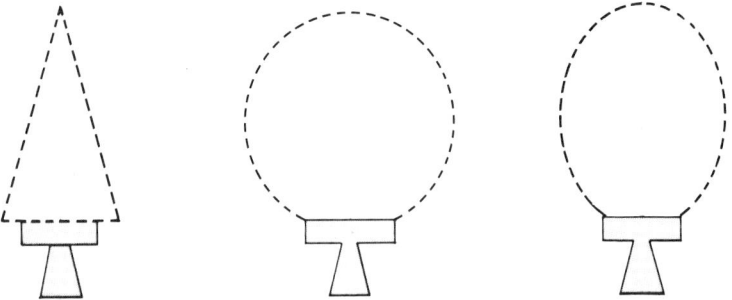

When a shape has two totally different halves it is asymmetrical. It may still look perfectly balanced because your eyes are equally attracted to either side of the centre but by different shapes.

Flowers can be arranged in an asymmetrical shape. The halves are not the same either side of the centre but they appear balanced because your eyes are equally attracted to both sides. The plant material on each side may also differ. You may place flowers on one side and a long branch on the other or two big flowers on one side and many small ones on the other. Your eyes should tell you

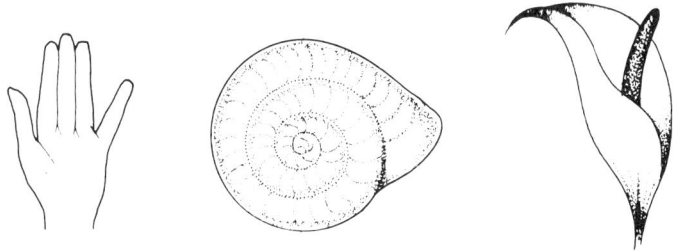

if the design looks lop-sided, and if so, you will need to add more plant material to the less eye-attracting side of the arrangement.

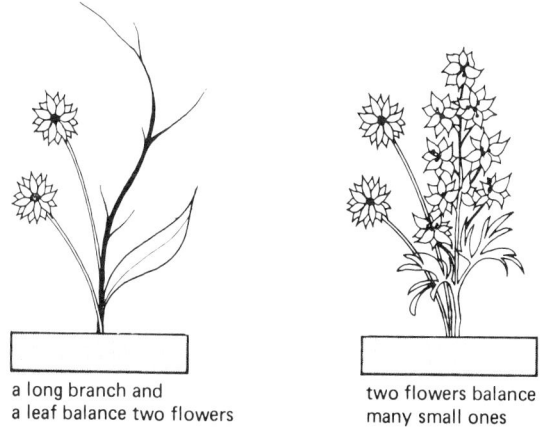

a long branch and
a leaf balance two flowers

two flowers balance
many small ones

A good test to see if an arrangement is balanced is to hold up a pencil so that when shutting one eye the pencil appears to go through the centre of the container. Now look to see if your eyes are equally attracted to both sides of the arrangement.

move this flower
to the other side

for better balance

So, a design may look lop-sided or well balanced. It can also look 'top-heavy', and about to tip over, because the container is too small for the number of flowers in it, or it can also be too small for the size of the flowers.

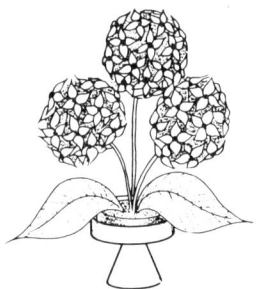

This can sometimes be corrected by adding a base which gives more visual weight to the bottom of the design.

Designs can also appear 'bottom-heavy' when there are not enough flowers in the arrangement for the size of the container or when they are too small for the container.

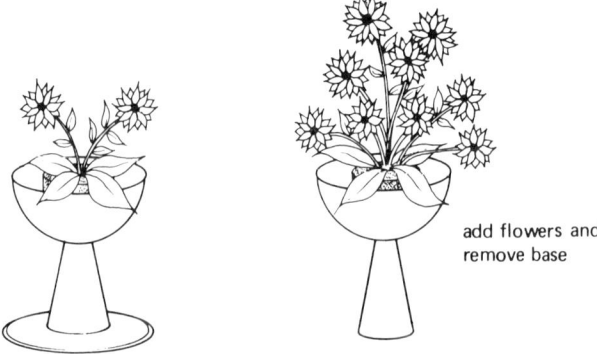

add flowers and remove base

Look at:
the balance of a painting when you hold up a pencil in the centre
symmetrical trees and trees leaning over in the wind
a pleasing shop window for the balance of goods

Try:
a symmetrical arrangement
a lop-sided design and then change it to one with better balance
an arrangement with many flowers at the top and then correct it by
adding a base or by removing some flowers
an arrangement of small flowers in a big container. See if the balance
is improved if the flowers are used on very long stems.

Special attractions

Good designs have parts that are more important than the other
parts. In a play some of the actors will have more important parts
than others. Well-designed gardens often have special features that
you look at first, such as specimen trees or a statue. When you speak
face to face with another person you usually look first at the eyes
because they are the focal point of the face. Although you will
glance at a person's nose and mouth sometimes, your eyes will
continue to return to the person's eyes. When you look at a painting
you will probably look at a figure before you look at the scenery and
in an abstract painting at the brightest colour or largest shape first.

The biggest flower in this design attracts your eyes first. The other
leaves, twigs and flowers are of lesser importance but necessary to
give interest to the design. However your eyes keep returning to
the big flower as the main feature.

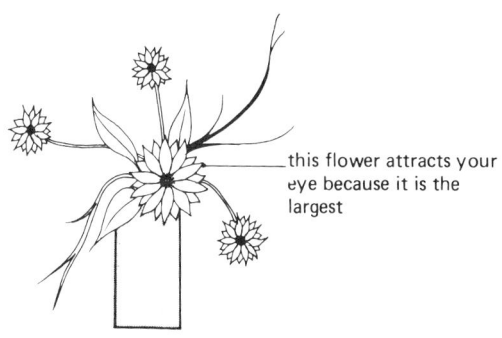

this flower attracts your
eye because it is the
largest

Good designs have areas of importance and areas of less importance. The important feature in a design can be in the centre of the arrangement, or elsewhere, as long as it appears balanced.

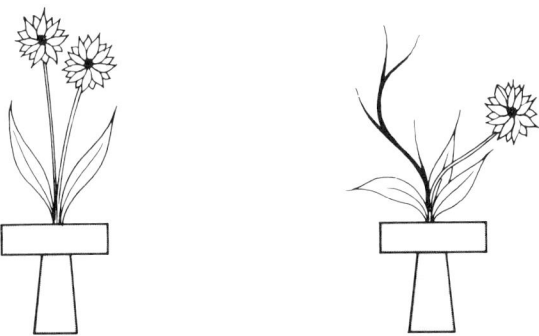

When you have made an arrangement and find that your eyes wander over it and never seem to rest anywhere, try adding two or three round flowers to give a special attraction or feature in the design.

two rounded flowers
added as a feature

Different qualities can make an object seem more important than other objects. For example bigger things look more important than smaller ones, brighter colours attract your eyes before duller ones, shiny surfaces before plain ones, rounded solid shapes before airy broken-up shapes.

Look at:
the important feature in a painting
the main feature in a garden
the more important actors in a play
the most important object in a shop window and decide why it is the most important.

Try:

making an arrangement of leaves and add two round flowers in
the centre

making an arrangement of leaves and adding a rosette of leaves in
the centre

making a design of flowers in one colour and then adding two central
flowers in another colour

placing the important features at the top of the design

Display

The way in which a flower arrangement, a sculpture or a painting
is displayed is important. When an object is crowded by other
objects it cannot be seen clearly. But when adequate space is given
around each object then you can enjoy and admire each one better.
Too many objects together give a junk-shop appearance, so it is better
to select a few and display them well.

One or two objects can be too few and look lonely.

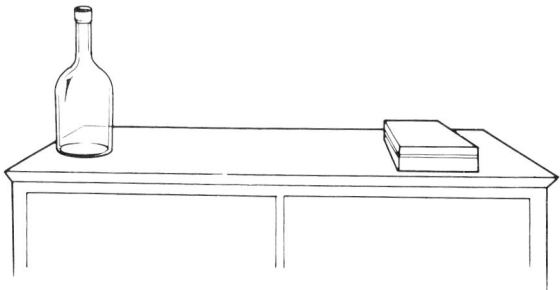

Objects of the same height look uninteresting.

These objects are of different height, have space around and can be seen easily.

You may find it easier to make an arrangement in the place for which it is intended. In this way you can fit the size and shape to the available space. No mess is made if you spread newspaper or polythene on the floor, for the plant material and any waste bits.

Look at:
the way other people group objects in their homes
the setting for a play in a theatre
advertisements
shop windows for the grouping of goods
pictures in magazines for the way people and things are grouped

Try:

re-arranging one of your own display shelves

a flower arrangement in your room in a new position

arranging several objects such as kitchen utensils, moving them about until you are pleased with the grouping

a flower arrangement on one side of a baking dish with water showing on the other side

an arrangement next to a painting or ornament so that they complement each other

cutting out your furniture to scale on squared paper and placing it on a floor plan of your room, trying the furniture in different positions

5. Style

Style is the manner in which something is made and flowers can be arranged in a variety of styles in the same way as furniture and clothes. The rounded, bouquet style of massed flowers in a bowl is a design that has been made for many centuries in the western world. Arrangements of bare branches and a few flowers and leaves are a new style for the West and have been inspired by the arrangements of China and Japan which tend to be simpler and more restrained. The way of making mass and line designs has already been described. There are other styles to try.

Landscape designs

A landscape design is a copy of a natural scene and so it is not difficult or expensive to make. It may look like a small part of a lakeside, a woodland, a garden, a mountain, a stream or a moor. You can gather material for a landscape on a visit to any of these places. For example there may be ferns, rushes, grasses and bulrushes growing near a lake and there will probably be a few stones in the water. Take a few of each home and arrange them on a pinholder at one side of a baking dish full of water. Leave some of the water showing and use the stones to cover the pinholder. You have then made a landscape design.

A scene by the side of a stream can be made in the same way. A landscape of the sea-shore can be made with a piece of driftwood, a heap of sand, shells, small feathers and a few grasses from the sand-hills, on a base. A woodland scene can be made with foliage, ferns, branches, pine cones and moss. A small piece of bark can be used to cover the mechanics and everything can be assembled on a crosscut of tree-trunk. The atmosphere of a mountainside can be recalled with heather or gorse, stones and moss on a piece of slate or stone. In spring, small bunches of primroses, bluebells, snowdrops and violets from a florist can be added to a woodland or garden scene.

A landscape design giving the atmosphere of a lake-side, using bulrushes, ferns and irises held on a pinholder in a tin concealed by stones. The water can be seen and helps the atmosphere.

A pot-et-fleur of small plants with a separated spray of single chrysanthemums supported on a pinholder in a small tin placed in the front of the bowl.

Tuck the stems into a small tin of water concealed by driftwood, bark or moss.

It is usually better to unite your grouping of plant material either in a shallow container or on a base. Bases of natural materials such as wood, slate and stone look more in keeping with the landscape style than fabric bases.

A pot-et-fleur

This is a style that combines growing plants with cut flowers and it is useful and economical in winter when flowers are scarce. You need:
  a container not less than about six inches (15 cm) deep to hold compost in which the roots of the plants can grow. Soup tureens, old saucepans, plastic or pottery bowls and Victorian wash-bowls are all suitable.
  gravel from a builder's yard or your driveway, about four handfuls
  charcoal, a small bag can be obtained from a garden centre
  compost, a bag of John Innes potting compost number 2 can be obtained in a polythene bag from a garden centre
  plants, about four small ones with contrasting foliage (not flowering plants which have a short life). Ask your florist or nurseryman for plants that like the same conditions and can be grouped successfully together. For example a hydrangea likes a lot of water and cannot grow in the same pot as a Mother-in-law's tongue (*Sansevieria*) which has to be kept very dry.

Method of planting

Wash the container and place the gravel in the bottom. Sprinkle the charcoal over the top and add about three inches of compost. Add the plants on top of the compost. Take them out of their pots in the following way:
Squeeze a plastic pot all round.
Turn it upside down so that the plant drops into your hand – if it does not, then knock it on the side of a table.

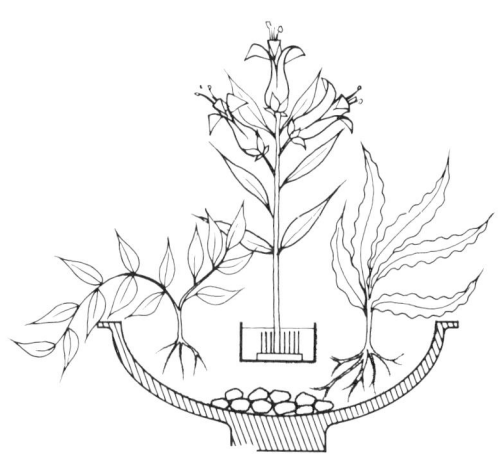

Place the plants including the soil in which they were growing into your big container.

Fill up the gaps between the plants with John Innes number 2 leaving a space in the centre. Press the compost all around the roots but do not press the roots or you may damage them. There should be at least one inch (2·5 cm) of space between the compost and the rim of the container for watering the plants. If the compost is level with the top of the container, the water will run off on to your furniture. Water until the compost feels really damp (not mushy) and then leave for two weeks without water so that the plants settle down.

Adding flowers

Place a small food tin containing a pinholder and water, or soaked plastic foam, into the space in the centre of the compost. Place a few flowers into it amongst the plants. When the flowers die you can replace them with fresh flowers or leave the growing plants on their own for a while.

Care of the plants

Water about every ten to fourteen days giving the compost a good soak, but never water if the compost feels wet. Fill the space between the compost and the rim of the container with water. A good soak infrequently is far better than a daily dribble of water. Spray the plants every week or two with a sprayer, obtainable from a garden centre. Give less water from October to March. Plants can be replaced whenever necessary, but they usually thrive when growing together.

Geometrical designs, seen in a triangle, a Hogarth curve and a crescent, are so called because they follow recognizable ge ometric shapes, and are described below.

A triangle

This is a classical design of massed flowers which makes a change from the rounded bouquet style. It is usually placed in front of a wall. The term triangle is used for this design because it is roughly the shape of the arrangement if seen in silhouette. 'Triangle' refers to the outline. In practice, the design has depth unlike a triangle drawn on paper. It looks better when arranged in a container with a stem, such as an urn, because the lower flowers can be seen more clearly. For this design you need:

a stemmed container

mechanics, which should be plastic foam because a triangle is difficult to make on a pinholder

plant material, a few pieces (leaves or flowers) with straight stems and a few with curved stems

flowers, two or three larger, round ones and a few smaller ones

leaves, about five plain leaves for covering the foam.

Method

Place a block of foam into the container so that it stands about two inches above the rim.

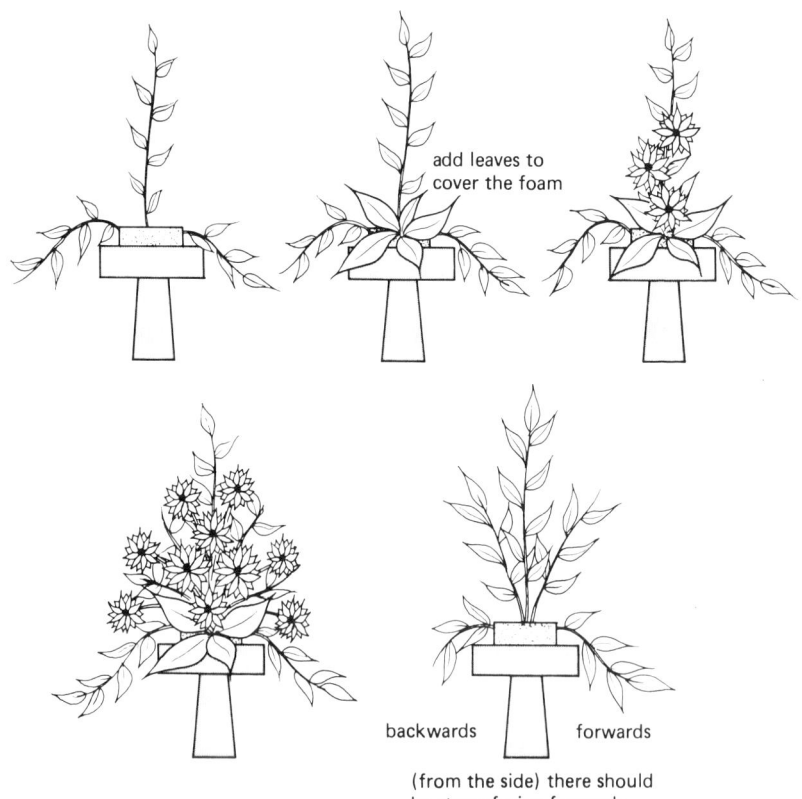

add leaves to cover the foam

backwards   forwards

(from the side) there should be stems facing forwards and backwards

A triangular arrangement of dried flowers including globe thistle, larkspur, sea holly, ferns and daisy type helipterums with wire stems.

A gentle Hogarth curve of roses and rose foliage with Kaffir lilies supported by foam on a foam anchor. The S shape can be turned either way.

Put a long straight stem in the centre of the foam about two thirds of the way back. The tip of this stem makes the highest point of the triangle.

Then place two shorter, curved stems on either side of the container, flowing downwards. These complete the three points of the triangle and all the other stems should be kept within this framework.

Add depth by placing short stems at right angles in the centre front, and centre back, of the design. All stems should appear to radiate from a central point in the middle of the block of foam.

Cover the foam with leaves before adding two larger flowers in the centre as features.

Add other plant material as you wish. The arrangement can look solid, like a cone, or spacious. Turn the outside flowers on their

Hogarth curve

crescent

a line arrangement in a circle   a mass arrangement in a circle

sides as for the bouquet style, so that the flowers seem to turn around an imaginary central axis.

A Hogarth curve

William Hogarth, the painter drew a line like this S and declared that it was the most beautiful line that could be drawn. It can easily be followed in plant material if you use curved stems, and a container with a tall stem so that the flowers have room to flow down one side. You need:

a stemmed container
a block of foam
plant material, with long curved stems
flowers, several larger round ones, and a few smaller ones
foliage to fill in and cover the foam

Method

Fit the foam into the container, making sure that about two inches (5 cm) stands above the rim. Place one long curving stem on one side of the top of the foam, curving up and inwards. Place another curving stem in the opposite side of the foam curving down and inwards. This gives an S shape.

Cover the foam with leaves and then add the remaining plant material with the larger flowers in the centre, keeping to the original S shape. It is not possible to make this style on a pinholder or with straight-stemmed plant material.

A crescent

This is a soft flowing design that looks pretty in a very tall, stemmed container. It is a useful style to make when you have a lot of floppy stems that will not stand up well. You need:

a stemmed container
a block of foam
flowers, two or three larger and a few smaller ones
foliage for filling in and covering the foam

Method

Place two long, curving stems to flow downwards in the shape of a crescent on each side of the container. Add some shorter stems also spraying downwards to make the first stems seem less isolated. Cover the foam with leaves and add the largest flowers in the centre and smaller ones further out, still following the lines flowing down. It is not possible to make this design on a pinholder.

A crescent can be made in an upright position but stems with a natural curve should be used. A wine glass on a wooden mat holds foam to support daffodils, leaves and winter jasmine.

A free-form design in a stoneware container filled with oddments of foam. One branch goes into the foam and another rests on top of the container.

Free-form designs

Arrangements do not need to be made in a geometric shape. Plant material can be placed in a design in any way that you like. It is then free of geometric form and abbreviated it becomes 'free-form'. Some people call a style 'modern' when it has no strong geometric outline but this is a rather broad description. Simple designs with two or three branches and a few flowers are free-form. More complicated arrangements may also be free-form. You can make this design with any type of plant material but more successful designs are made with some line plant material, two or three rounded flowers (points) and a few in-between shapes in foliage. You can

use a pinholder or foam as the mechanics and any type of container, but one that is clearly traditional is not as suitable as a simple modern style.

Method

Place a piece of plant material on one side of the container. This gives a lop-sided appearance so add another piece on the other side, keeping the stem ends close together on the mechanics. Continue adding plant material to either side of the container until you feel you have enough in the design. The arrangement should appear balanced even though you have different plant material either side of the centre. If it is not balanced remove something or add something until it looks right. Do not try to follow an outline shape.

The number of free-form designs that you can make is infinite because you can use such a variety of plant materials in an endless number of shapes. They suit more modern homes and use less plant material than massed arrangements.

A dried cone

A cone of dried plant material can be made as an almost permanent decoration. This is something the family also enjoy doing. A cone of plastic foam for dried plant material can be bought at a florist's. Collect dried seedheads and flowers and some small preserved leaves. You also need pins.

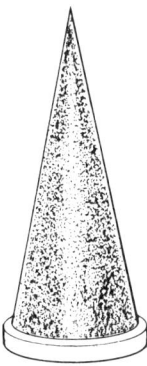

Method

A brown foam cone is better if obtainable. If you can only get green, then cover it first with preserved leaves by placing pins through the leaves into the cone to cover it closely.

Then add dried flowers on wire stems by pushing the wire into the cone. Each wire should be about an inch (2·5 cm) in length. Some seedheads, such as poppy, have strong stems which can be pushed into the foam easily. It does not matter if the stems go through the covering leaves. You can group the plant material in varieties or make concentric circles or scatter the flowers and seedheads anywhere. If you place the completed cone on a low dish, with a few preserved leaves at the base, it looks more finished.

Fruit arrangements

Fruit can be arranged pleasingly in a bowl, or on a base, to make a quick arrangement for the centre of a dining table, especially when flowers are expensive .

Fruit is always available and is economical because it can be eaten afterwards. Group varieties together after selecting a number

Fruit for a table centrepiece including gourds, apples, grapes, peppers and a pineapple held in place by cocktail sticks and meat skewers.

of varying colours, shapes and textures. To prevent the fruit from rolling about, place half of a clean cocktail stick into one piece of fruit and the other half into another fruit. A few preserved leaves can be added to fill up the gaps.

Gift arrangements

Take an arrangement of flowers instead of a bunch of cut flowers to a friend as a gift. Most people are delighted to receive flowers already arranged and it will have given you practice in arranging. As a hospital gift this is especially welcome because it saves time for nurses and other helpers. A plastic saucer containing foam is inexpensive, or you can use any plastic dish, previously sold with food, and add foam to it. Small baskets and containers are also sold by florists for this purpose.

An arrangement in the manner of a Flemish flower painting

There are times when you can only pick flowers in the garden in ones and twos. This often happens in late autumn when you can pick one rose, a dahlia, and so on. If you study one of the paintings of flowers by the Flemish old masters you will see that they mixed flowers together in ones and twos of a kind. You can see original paintings in the National Gallery in London, the Ashmolean Museum in Oxford and other art galleries. Reproductions can be seen on postcards, Christmas and gift cards. Study the way the artist has combined the flowers and the colours he has used, especially for the background, and look at his method of turning flowers so that you can see the sides and backs of them.

Christmas arrangements

Most people like to have Christmas arrangements or decorations, in their homes. Evergreens such as holly, fir and cedar look attractive with red roses or carnations and holly berries. Yellow-berried holly can sometimes be found and this is lovely with gold carnations or chrysanthemums, if red does not suit your room.

Gold, copper and silver spray paint can be bought at chain stores to colour preserved leaves. It is a good idea to preserve extra leaves for this purpose. Each colour of paint can be used separately or you can spray one on top of another for varying effects. Spray

A simple combination of carnations, roses and foliage can be arranged in a plastic saucer holding foam, to be given as a gift.

An arrangement of mixed flowers in many colours in an urn. It resembles a Flemish flower painting.

lightly so that the leaves are not entirely covered to give a less artificial and more interesting effect. Flowers or baubles on wires can be combined with the painted leaves. Pine cones spray well and can be combined in clusters with leaves. Seedheads are also attractive when sprayed with paint.

Method of spraying

Hold the can about two to three feet away from the plant material when spraying. To avoid painting anything nearby, the plant material can be placed inside the upturned lid of a cardboard box, or on newspaper. The paint dries almost at once but leave it for a few minutes before handling.

spraying leaves

Glittering

Tubes of glitter can be bought at chain stores and stationers. Sprinkle it on to plant material that has just been sprayed before the paint dries. Do this over an old plate or a piece of newspaper so that you collect surplus glitter. Clear varnish can also be bought in spray cans and this can be used in place of coloured paint to hold the glitter. When you want to use glitter thickly, squeeze clear adhesive on to the plant material and scatter glitter on to it. Alternatively put the glitter in a polythene bag. Add the plant material with touches of adhesive on it. Shake the bag and the glitter will stick to the adhesive.

Artificial snow

This can look wintry, sprayed on to evergreens arranged with white chrysanthemums. Aerosol cans of snow can be bought at chain stores. Spray from a distance of two or three feet (60–90 cm), protecting the surroundings with newspaper. Immediately after 'snowing' turn the can upside down and continue spraying for a few seconds to clear the nozzle, which can easily become blocked.

Oil lamps and candles can be combined with flowers and leaves to give a Christmas atmosphere but be careful about naked flames near to dry plant material because you may cause a fire. Bows give a

An arrangement for Christmas of variegated holly, carnations, snowberries, pine cones and baubles placed on the end of small sticks. A trivet holds a small bowl of plastic foam. The candle is pushed into this before the plant material.

festive appearance and Christmas ribbon is easily available. Buy one and a half yards (1·5 m) of one or two inch (2–5 cm) width ribbon.

Method of making a bow

Spread the length of ribbon on a table; hold the two ends in your hands and cross your hands over. This crosses the ribbon into a wide loop. Gather the centre of this loop together with the place

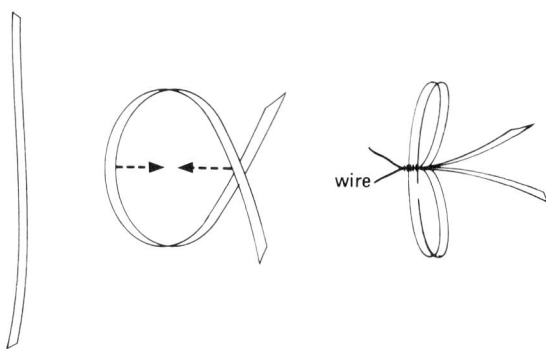

where the ribbons cross. Twist a stub wire tightly round and you have a bow with long ends. The wire can be used to secure the bow to your Christmas arrangement.

Your own styles

It is much more satisfying to create styles of your own than to copy those of other people. Some imitation is necessary when you begin to learn flower arrangement but you will gradually be able to try your own ideas as you become more confident about the basic skill of supporting plant material in a container. Take time to play with flowers and leaves and to know their ways. Look for special interest and beauty in plant material that you want to display well. Try different colour schemes, collect new containers and accessories, look at design in other crafts, search for materials everywhere, analyse other people's arrangements. Sometimes you will feel successful when you try something new and at other times you may be disappointed. This is part of learning.

6. Taking It Further

Assessing your own arrangements

You learn more about any subject if you are able to have your progress assessed so that you are aware of faults and ways in which you could make improvements. If you know an experienced flower arranger or a designer in another craft it is helpful to listen to comments. You should not mind any suggestions. Although you may not agree at first, think about the comments and give other ideas a trial. You may find that you have learnt something, or alternatively, be more convinced that you were right in the first place. So assessment is helpful either way.

When no one is available who knows any more than you do about design, try assessing your own arrangements. It is wise to make an arrangement quickly and to return to it later when you will look at it afresh. You can assess the things you like about it and those you feel could be improved. Most plant material has a short life and it is better not to make changes in an arrangement but to bear them in mind for the next time that you arrange flowers. To help you assess your own arrangements, ask yourself the following questions:

1 *Container and arrangement*

Are the flowers and stems firm in the container? If they wobble, what can be done to stop it? Does the arrangement *look* firm? If it looks lop-sided and likely to overbalance, what might improve it?

Is the plant material closely related to the container in shape, texture and colour?

Does the plant material seem more important than the container?

2 *Overall design*

Are flowers, leaves, container and base related in size?

Would a base improve the design because there is a lot of plant material in a small container? Have you avoided the danger of making the base 'bottom-heavy'?

Is there space around each piece of plant material? If the design looks crowded, can you analyse why?

Are there main features in the design, such as two larger, more important flowers?

Are there contrasts of rough and smooth surfaces in the design?

Have damaged leaves, faded flowers and broken stems been cut away?

3 *Arrangement and surroundings*

Do the colours go well together and seem attractive in the room?

Does the arrangement suit its surroundings in colour, size and purpose?

Is the arrangement clearly displayed and in harmony with the objects nearby?

Assessing other people's arrangements

It is helpful to look at other people's flower arrangements for ideas and for comparison with your own. There are different opportunities for doing this:

Look at illustrations of arrangements in books from a library, newspapers and magazines. Decide why you like some and not others.

Visit local flower arrangement shows and horticultural shows where flower arrangements are included. Study the designs and decide which you like. Read the judges' comment cards and see if you agree. Study the prize-winners' exhibits and decide why they received prizes.

Look at arrangements and (silently) assess them in hotels, florists shops, shop windows and other people's homes. Decide if you could do better and how.

Opportunities for learning more

You can learn a lot on your own but sooner or later it is a good idea to have contact with other flower arrangers. This gives you ideas, helps you to learn more and enables you to discuss the subject with people who also enjoy it. There are flower arrangement clubs and classes that you can join.

Flower arrangement clubs

There are more than 1000 clubs in the British Isles so there is likely to be one in your neighbourhood. The members are men and women of all ages and backgrounds. Membership of clubs is rapidly increasing because flower arrangement is becoming increasingly popular. Addresses of clubs in your vicinity can be obtained from: The National Association of Flower Arrangement Societies of Great Britain (NAFAS), 21a, Denbigh Street, London SW1V 2HF, and sometimes local libraries or information centres can provide details.

Some clubs hold meetings in the afternoon and others hold them in the evening, normally once a month. Subscriptions vary between £2 and £5 a year according to the club. Usually at each meeting a visiting expert demonstrates flower arrangements and explains the designs, giving information about the plants, containers and accessories used in the demonstration. Clubs also hold social events, exhibitions and competitions in flower arrangement. There are usually classes for beginners as well as experienced flower arrangers. Many clubs have libraries of flower arrangement books and sales tables where you can buy containers, dried plant material, mechanics, Christmas supplies, bases and plants. Publications tables sell helpful books and leaflets on flower arrangement. You can also buy a magazine called *The Flower Arranger* which is published quarterly and is obtainable through clubs and the office of NAFAS (address page 123). This journal includes articles to help you with flower arrangement and of interest to flower arrangers.

The official organization

NAFAS is the official organization of the flower arrangement movement in the British Isles. It works to promote a wide interest in flower arranging, gardening, and knowledge of plants. It has many international affiliates. The training and qualifying of demonstrators, judges and lecturers is undertaken and it liaises with the education authorities in the training and qualifying of flower arrangement teachers.

NAFAS holds national and area exhibitions and competitions

in flower arrangement and festivals in cathedrals and churches in various parts of the country. Residential and day conferences are held and there is a travel club for flower arrangers. Information about all these events is given in *The Flower Arranger* and at club meetings.

Classes

Classes in flower arrangement are held in local adult education centres and colleges of further education. Information about days, times and types of courses available can be obtained from the local college, library, or Council Education Officer. Details of classes are also published in many local newspapers at the beginning of September.

There are different types of course, held either in the evening or during the day. Leisure classes of varying lengths are given – some are of six weeks, some longer. The subjects include general flower arrangement, arranging church flowers, drying and preserving plant material, Christmas decorations and so on. If you wish to make a serious study of flower arrangement, and gain a recognized, national qualification to prove you have reached a required standard, there are courses leading to a City and Guilds of London Institute certificate. The part 1 course assumes no previous knowledge in general flower arrangement and takes three hundred hours, at times arranged by the college mounting the course. Part 2 taking two hundred hours is for more advanced flower arrangers. The courses include flower arrangement, design, horticulture and botany.

Entering flower arrangement shows

Entering flower arrangement shows will help you to improve your skill. It may be necessary to join a club to do this although some shows, usually horticultural shows, have classes open to anyone. Write or telephone the secretary of the show a few weeks before and ask for a schedule. This gives the regulations of the show and should be read carefully. If you join a flower club, or a class, you will be given help over the procedure for entering shows. If you feel nervous think to yourself that there will be many people feeling the same way who are also inexperienced.

Winning your first prize in a show is exciting and gives you more confidence. If you do not win anything there is no doubt that you will have still learnt a lot. This comes from watching other flower arrangers, looking at the exhibits, comparing one arrangement with another, studying the prizewinners and talking to other exhibitors. A show widens your experience and stimulates your interest. You will find that most accomplished flower arrangers have entered many shows in the early stages of learning and now attribute much of their success to competitive work.

Other things to learn

Although you should have learnt a great deal after reading this book and can no longer be termed a beginner, there is more to learn if you wish. The subject of flower arrangement is now a big one, with many facets, and new ideas are constantly appearing.

Combining accessories with flowers

Flowers may be combined with attractive figurines, plates, bottles, basketry, metal and other ornaments. Some practice is needed in melding these successfully with flowers. Accessories are often used in interpretative designs.

Interpretative designs

These are arrangements that interpret a mood or tell a story. The flowers you arrange in your home are called decorative designs and they are made to enhance their setting. Interpretative designs use plant material symbolically and are not necessarily attractive. For example you could interpret 'gaiety' in flowers using pinks and reds. You could also interpret 'sadness' in dull colours with drooping plant material. A landscape arrangement is interpretative as it 'tells a story' and describes a scene in nature. This type of flower arrangement is sometimes asked for in a flower arrangement show where the exhibits are judged for the message they convey, rather than their decorative quality. It is interesting to see how competitors interpret the same subject in different ways.

Pressed flower pictures

Pictures of pressed flowers are permanent decorations to make for your home. The plant material is pressed flat in a flower press, or between books, for several months until it is paper thin and dry. It is

An arrangement of hyacinth and contorted hazel branches with honesty leaves hiding a tin containing a pinholder. This is an attractive way of arranging any flowers with short stems. The figurine is an accessory to add interest and a cork mat unites everything.

assembled into a design to place under glass. This is an absorbing interest for winter evenings.

Swags and plaques

These are decorations of plant material made for hanging up in your home. A swag is not mounted on a visible backing but a plaque is mounted on a backing that can be seen, such as a fabric-covered board. They can be made with fresh or dried plant material.

Drying plant material with a desiccant

Flowers can be dried by means of a desiccant which is a substance that withdraws and retains water from plant material. This is suitable for compact flowers, such as big roses and pom-pom dahlias, and only takes a few days. The results are fragile but with care can be used in dry rooms for many weeks.

Church flower arrangements and festivals

Arranging flowers in churches is very rewarding and designs are often made on a large scale for festivals. The supports for big arrangements must be carefully made and there is much to learn about the mechanics. You can also learn how to organize a church flower festival.

Pedestal arrangements

This term refers to a large arrangement made on the top of a stand on the floor. It may measure any height above about four feet. This is a useful decoration to be able to do, for special occasions such as weddings.

Period arrangements

Flower arrangements are as old as civilization and flowers have been cut and placed in water, all over the world, for centuries. They have been used both decoratively and symbolically and make a fascinating study because they involve history and past cultures. They also give ideas for present-day styles.

Abstract designs

Twentieth-century influences have led to abstract art and this has introduced another chapter into the book of flower arrangement. In abstract designs plant material is used more for its design qualities and is assembled in an unrealistic manner. Normally flower arrangers work with forms already created by nature whereas potters, painters, weavers and other designers work with 'raw' materials such as clay, paint and textiles in which they create their own forms. Flower arrangers normally use their medium without changing it except for cutting, grooming, trimming and sometimes altering the colour by preservation and drying. However, when creating abstract designs, plant material is used more as a 'raw' medium and altered by painting, cutting and so on. These styles suit modern rooms.

Plant material

Useful plant material can be added to the garden to give you a greater variety of flowers, leaves, fruits and seedheads to cut all the year round. There are also many more plants to preserve and dry and a search can continue for driftwood. Some flowers need special conditioning and there is more to learn about growing and about plant names.

Design

Although you already know something about designing including scale, balance and making special features, there is more to learn. The principles of contrast, dominance, proportion, rhythm and harmony are fascinating to study. Colour can be an unending interest and harmony and unity can be studied. Experiments can be made with other media.

Making equipment

It is useful to be able to make your own containers, bases and accessories in flower arrangement, pottery and woodwork classes. You can also learn how to adapt various objects to use as containers. Accessories can be created from different new materials and backgrounds can be made to place behind your arrangements to display them well in shows.

A notebook

You will find it helpful to begin to keep a notebook in which you can also draw rough sketches, write reminders and so on. It is also a useful place to keep press cuttings and pictures of flower arrangements.

Future activities

As you become a more knowledgeable and experienced flower arranger there are activities in which you can take part in addition to making your own home more attractive. You may:

Volunteer to arrange the flowers sent to a hospital. Write to the matron or administrator to offer your help. This is rewarding and relieves the nurses to do other work. It is unlikely to be a paid job.

Volunteer to arrange the flowers in an old people's home. Write to the matron about this.

Offer help in arranging the flowers in a local church.

Train to be a demonstrator of flower arrangement through your own flower arrangement club. Training is only a few days in duration but you should know your subject well before taking the required test. A demonstrator, when she has passed a test and been placed on a list of demonstrators which is distributed to clubs, can charge a fixed travelling rate, the cost of flowers and a fee, depending on experience and popularity.

Train to be a judge of flower arrangement through your own flower club. After a few days' training a test is given, but again you should know your subject well before taking the test. Judges are paid expenses and a small fee for judging the flower arrangement classes in competitive shows.

Train to become a part-time teacher of flower arrangement in a college that provides adult education. It is necessary to obtain a City and Guilds of London Institute certificate for the part 1 and part 2 flower arrangement courses before taking teacher training. The part-time teachers' course then lasts one or two years depending on the hours of attendance each week. There are hourly rates of pay laid down for this type of work. Teachers are also needed in hospitals as part of the therapeutic work, in women's prisons and in homes for the mentally or physically handicapped.

Become a voluntary administrator in a flower club and do secretarial, accounting and other organizational work. Committees often need members to run shows, sales tables, libraries and so on.

Apply to a hotel for regular, paid work in arranging the hotel flowers. Some large offices also employ flower arrangers.

Do freelance work arranging party flowers in people's homes and elsewhere for a negotiated fee.

Bibliography

The Flower Arranger, a quarterly magazine published by The National Association of Flower Arrangement Societies of Great Britain (NAFAS) obtainable through the National Office of NAFAS, 21a Denbigh Street, London SW1V 2HF. This publication gives help and provides articles of interest to all flower arrangers.

A series of education leaflets for beginners, concerning the skills of conditioning, preserving, drying plant material and other useful subjects. These are published at low cost and available from the address of NAFAS above.

Planting for Pleasure by Jean Taylor, published by Stanley Paul, concerns gardening for flower arrangers with a useful list of plants.

Practical Flower Arranging by Jean Taylor, published by The Hamlyn Group. A comprehensive, basic book for flower arrangers, with many illustrations.

Creative Flower Arrangement by Jean Taylor, published by Stanley Paul. A detailed book for serious students providing basic information on design and suggestions to increase creativity and originality.

Flowers in Church by Jean Taylor, published by Mowbray and concerning all aspects of arranging church flowers including festivals and special occasions.

Design for Flower Arrangers by Dorothy Riester, published by Van Nostrand Reinhold, an advanced book on design for flower arrangers.

A History of Flower Arrangement by Julia S. Berrall, published by Thames and Hudson and concerning flower arrangement throughout history, with many illustrations.

The Collingridge Book of Dried and Pressed Flowers by Jane Derbyshire and Renée Burgess, published by The Hamlyn Group.

The Complete Book of Flower Preservation by Geneal Condon, published by Robert Hale.

Index

Compiled by Susan Kennedy

Page numbers in italics refer to photographs)